HOME
WINE
& BEER
MAKING

HOME
WINE
& BEER
MAKING
Ben Turner

TREASURE PRESS

First published in Great Britain by Park Lane Press
under the title *Home-made Wines and Beers*

This edition published in 1983 by Treasure Press
59 Grosvenor Street
London W1

Reprinted 1985

© 1979 Ben Turner

This book was designed and produced by
George Rainbird Ltd
40 Park Street, London W1Y 4DE

ISBN 0 907812 31 7

Printed in Hong Kong

Acknowledgment:

The publishers would like to thank Derek Pearman
of W. R. Loftus, Charlotte Street, London W1 for his kindness in providing
materials and equipment used in the photography for this book.

CONTENTS

WARNING

When dissolving Campden tablets in citric acid take care to avoid the Sulphur Dioxide which is produced, especially if you suffer from a bronchial condition.

EASY MADE WINES FROM KITS

Anyone who has never made wine before is strongly recommended to start by making up a few kits of concentrated grape juice of whatever style suits your taste. This gives you a quick understanding of the techniques, the need for sterilising equipment, the fermentation process, removing the clear wine from the sediment by siphoning, and so on. Perhaps equally important, it produces a wine that is drinkable only three months after opening the can! There are some kits available the manufacturers of which claim that the wine is ready for drinking at three weeks, and at least one, after only fourteen days! These manufacturers would not disagree, however, that their wines improve with keeping a little longer. Between six and twelve months from the start of fermentation the wines, especially the whites and rosés, are at their best. The reds improve even more with yet longer storage.

Concentrated grape juice has been available for nearly 100 years. Indeed, millions of bottles of wine have been made from it every year and sold commercially as British wine, mostly of sherry or port style. Since the late 1950s, small packs have been marketed for the use of home winemakers. As competition increased from new manufacturers and distributors, the range of styles widened. Today, you can buy a different kit to simulate almost every wine style in Europe.

Mostly they are available in cans or polythene bottles sufficient to produce six bottles of wine, but larger containers are also available to make up to thirty bottles at a time. With increasing expertise the quality has improved and most kits now produce an acceptable wine usually as good as what is sometimes unkindly called 'supermarket plonk'. Quite often it is a good deal better. On the whole, the white table wines seem to be slightly better than the reds, but this is a matter of individual taste, skill and the choice of pack. What cannot be denied is that the kits sell in their scores of thousands, week by week, throughout the year and give a great deal of pleasure to millions of people.

At first, France and Germany refused to supply grape juice for concentrating and the manufacturers used Spanish and Cypriot grape juice, but now Italian and French grape juice is also used. Manufacturers blend the different concentrates and add flavourings to produce their different styles. The Danes, surprisingly, also have a large stake in this market with flavoured fruit concentrates (especially apple) to produce traditional grape wine styles, red, white and rosé.

The ingredients

The normal kits usually consist of just a can or bottle of concentrated grape juice with precise step-by-step instructions printed on the label describing the method to be followed in making up the contents. Some additional sugar is required as well as water and, of course, some yeast. Campden tablets are also needed for sterilising the equipment and adding to the wine when fermentation has finished.

'The Three-Week Kits', on the other hand, are often made from fruits other than grapes and contain in addition to the concentrate, a number of different packets of chemicals, for sterilising the equipment, for fermenting the diluted concentrate, for fining the young wine and stabilising it against further fermentation. Only sugar and water has to be provided by the winemaker.

An assortment of concentrated grape juices

What you need

Only very basic equipment is required to make up a kit. It consists of:
1. a large glass jar usually called a 'demijohn' or 'gallon jar' (although many of them hold 5 litres ($8\frac{1}{2}$ pints));
2. a bored cork bung to fit the jar and an airlock to fit into the hole in the bung;
3. a plastic funnel and a piece of plastic tubing about a metre long;
4. six wine bottles and corks.

A number of firms market a 'Beginners Kit' in a carton containing the equipment mentioned, a can of concentrate, a sachet of yeast, sometimes a bag of sugar and a sachet of Campden tablets. All you are asked to provide in addition is the water! The equipment can be used over and over again and so, spread over its period of usability, the cost per bottle is infinitesimal.

Once started, however, you quickly find that you could do with some extra jars, bottles, corks, airlocks and bungs without holes as well as some with them. You may also feel that you need some labels and even foil caps to add that professional finish to your bottles. A few bottle cartons are also handy for storage. A polythene bin in which to mix the concentrate and water is another very useful piece of equipment, although a large bowl or jug will do instead at this stage. A wooden or plastic spoon, although required for stirring, is usually part of normal kitchen equipment and need not be obtained solely for making wine.

What to do

The first thing to do is dissolve one Campden tablet in a cupful of cold water. The tablets are sometimes hard but are easily crushed between two spoons and the powder soon dissolves in the water. If you have a packet of sterilising crystals provided with your kit, dissolve them in water as directed.

Assuming that your vessels are clean, rinse them in the solution. Pour it through the funnel into the jar, cover its mouth with the palm of your hand and shake it so that the solution wets every part of the inner surface several times. Empty out the solution and use it for soaking the bored cork.

Shake the can or container well, open it, remove two teaspoonfuls of grape concentrate and dissolve it in a cupful of cool, boiled water. Pour this into a bottle that has been

Basic equipment

7

Emptying the concentrate into the water in the jar

Adding the yeast to the must

Airlock fitted and jar labelled

sterilised as just described and add the wine yeast. Shake the bottle well to distribute the yeast, plug the neck with cotton wool and stand it in a warm place for a few hours.

Half fill the jar with cold boiled water and empty the contents of the can into it. Screw the airlock into the softened, bored cork, pour a little water into the airlock and fit the cork into the neck of the jar. As soon as the yeast solution can be seen to be fermenting, pour this into the jar. Refit the airlock, making sure that you have effected a good seal, label the jar and place it in a warm situation – a steady 21°C (70°F) is ideal.

The fermentation

Very soon the solution will become cloudy and bubbles will be seen rising in the jar. Eventually sufficient pressure will build up to force the gas up through the water in the airlock. The large lozenges of gas will burst with a plopping sound and will pass through the airlock in quick succession.

When most of the grape sugar in the concentrate has been converted into alcohol, the fermentation will slow down. This is the time to add the sugar. The quantity to add will vary with the type of wine and will be prescribed in the direction accompanying the kit.

Remove the airlock and pour some of the wine into a large jug, sterilised as already described. Add the requisite amount of white sugar and stir the mixture until the sugar is completely dissolved. Ordinary white granulated sugar is recommended. It will dissolve more quickly if it is first more finely ground in a blender or liquidiser, but this is not essential if such a facility is not available.

Return the sweetened wine to the jar and refit the airlock. Do not add dry sugar to the wine in the jar since this causes foaming. Furthermore, the sugar is then difficult to dissolve and may be left on the bottom of the jar. If a second quantity of sugar has to be added, repeat the process.

When all of the sugar has been added, top the jar up with cold boiled water to just above the bottom of the neck of the jar.

Leave the jar in the same warm place until fermentation has finished. This is indicated by the cessation of bubbles passing through the airlock. Now move the jar to the coolest place you can find and leave it there for a few days while it begins to clear.

Clearing the wine

This is where a second jar is useful, although not essential. The sediment in the fermentation jar, consisting mostly of dead yeast cells and fruit pulp, must be removed before it putrifies and taints the young wine. The easiest way to do this is to siphon the clearing wine into another sterilised jar or otherwise suitable container.

Sterilise the polythene tube, place the jar of wine on a table or work surface and the empty sterilised vessel on a chair or stool in such a position that the top of the receiving vessel is below the bottom of the wine. Remove the airlock, place one end of the siphon tube into the wine and suck the other end until the tube is full of wine. Pinch the end tightly and quickly place it into the neck of the receiving vessel. Release the pressure on the tube and the clearing wine will flow through the tube into the receiving vessel.

By holding the tube carefully in the wine so that it is never close to the sediment and by tilting the jar when necessary, almost all the wine can be transferred without disturbing the sediment. The sediment must be discarded, the jar washed out and sterilised and the clear wine returned to the jar. Top it up with cold boiled water – only a little will be needed if you have siphoned your wine carefully – and add one Campden tablet. This is most important. It protects the wine from over-oxidation and from infection. Place a softened, sterilised bung in the neck of the jar (see page 37), label it with the name of the contents and date and store it in a cool dark place.

The final stage

Keep an eye on the wine from time to time and as soon as it is crystal clear, siphon it from its second sediment into sterilised bottles. Fit softened, sterilised corks, label the bottles and store them in a cool place until the wine is at least three months old, longer if possible.

Different styles might require slight modifications. For example, a sweet wine would need two Campden tablets instead of one at the first siphoning and then a further two at the second siphoning when the wine is bright. The sugar to sweeten the wine is then added in the manner already described.

Different manufacturers might also express their instructions in a slightly different form. All are agreed, however, on the need for cleanliness and the sterilisation of equipment before use. All are agreed on the use of an airlock during fermentation and the addition of at least one Campden tablet at the first siphoning. Some manufacturers, however, recommend that dried yeast be added direct to the fermentation jar instead of re-activating it.

Making wine from kits is simple and successful. It is an excellent way for beginners to start. If you have never made wine before, start right now – from a kit.

Dissolving the sugar

Topping up

Corking the bottled wine

TRADITIONAL COUNTRY WINES

Wherever the vine did not grow, mankind endeavoured to make an alcoholic drink from the fruits, vegetables and other plants available to him.

The traditional quantities for making fruit wines were, and often still are, 2 kg (4 lb) fruit, 5 litres (4 quarts) of water and 2 kg (4 lb) sugar. These were fermented in an open tub or glazed crock under a slice of toast on which had been spread some baker's yeast.

The vessels were covered with butter muslin to keep out flies and dust. As the wine cleared, it was poured into earthenware jars and stored for a while.

Vessels were cleansed with boiling water and those who used wooden casks might burn a sulphur match in them to kill off 'the wild spirits' that would otherwise sour the wine.

Palates were less critical then than now. A slight haze was quite acceptable and was masked by a coloured glass or an opaque drinking vessel. There was little liking for dry wines and what would seem to us to be excessive sweetness was quite enjoyed. It also covered up unpleasant flavours that would otherwise have been more noticeable.

Country wines are still widely made, though with the aid of modern equipment and a better understanding of the principles. A polythene bin with a lid, some glass jars, bored bungs and airlocks, storage jars and stoppers, bottles and corks, a funnel, a siphon and a straining bag are the most important pieces of equipment. Some Campden tablets, pectic enzyme and wine yeasts are also needed. It is often helpful to add a little pectin-destroying enzyme to those fruits that make good jam. It ensures a better juice extraction and helps to prevent a haze in the finished wine.

All the recipes that follow make more than a jarful of wine. The surplus should be fermented in a smaller jar or large bottle beside the main jar (see page 33). It is especially useful for topping up the main jar after racking.

Although the yeast can be added direct to the must it is better to re-activate it first. Instructions on how to do this are given on page 29.

Fruit wines

Blackberry Wine

Freshly picked ripe blackberries

Pectin-destroying enzyme

Campden tablets

White sugar

Yeast

Stalk, wash and thoroughly crush the blackberries in a suitable vessel, add some pectic

enzyme – quantities given on the packet – and one crushed Campden tablet for every 2 kg (4 lb) of fruit. Cover the vessel closely and leave it in a warm room for two days.

Strain out the pulp and press it dry, discard. Measure the juice and stir in 1.5 kg (3 lb) of sugar for every 5 litres (1 gallon). This will increase the volume by 1 litre (1¾ pints) for every 1.5 kg (3 lb) of sugar used.

When the sugar is well dissolved, stir in an activated wine yeast and pour the must into fermentation jars. Fill the jars completely and cover each one with an inverted cup or basin.

Stand the vessel on a tray and leave in a warm room, say around 18°C (65°F), fermentation will soon start.

At first, the yeast and fruit pulp will 'boil over' and run down the outside of the vessel into the tray. After a while, however, the fermentation will quieten down. Wash the neck and outside of the jar, top it up with any surplus juice or with a little cold boiled water, fit an airlock and continue the fermentation.

When the water in the airlock remains still and the wine begins to clear, siphon it from its sediment into a clean jar, top it up, add one Campden tablet, bung tight and store in a cool dark place for one year. The wine is a rich red, full flavoured and strong in alcohol. Sweeten it further, if necessary, before serving.

Apple Wine

6 kg (12 lb) mixed apples
Pectic enzyme and Campden tablets
5 litres (1 gallon) cold water
Champagne wine yeast
White sugar

Use as many different varieties of apples as you can get. Three-quarters of them should be eating apples, the rest should be cooking apples. Some hard pears and quinces may be included. The latter improve the bouquet and flavour.

Dissolve the pectic enzyme and one Campden tablet in the water. Wash and crush the apples or cut them up into small pieces and drop them into the water. Cover the vessel and leave it in a warm place for 24 hours.

In the meantime, activate a wine yeast and next day add it to the apples. Ferment on the pulp for four days keeping the pulp submerged or press it down twice daily. Keep the vessel covered but allow the gas to escape.

Strain out and press the pulp as dry as you can, discard and then stir in 1 kg (2 lb) sugar per 5 litres (1 gallon).

Continue the fermentation under an airlock. When no more bubbles rise, rack the wine from its sediment and add 1 Campden tablet per

5 litres (1 gallon). Fine with a tablespoonful of milk well mixed in. Keep for 6–9 months.

This makes a dry light table wine. A stronger, sweeter wine can be made with 1.5 kg (3 lb) sugar per 5 litres (1 gallon).

John Downie and the Siberian crab apples also make excellent wine.

Gooseberry Wine

2 kg (4 lb) gooseberries	Pectic enzyme and Campden tablets
1.5 kg (3 lb) white sugar	Wine yeast
5 litres (1 gallon) water	

Wash, top and tail the gooseberries, pour on hot water to soften them and when cool crush them with your hands.

Add the pectic enzyme and one crushed Campden tablet and leave covered for 24 hours.

Stir in one-third of the sugar and an activated yeast and ferment on the pulp for three days keeping the fruit submerged and the bin covered.

Strain out and press the fruit dry, discard the pulp and stir in the rest of the sugar and ferment out under an airlock.

Rack into sterilised containers, add one Campden tablet and store for 9–12 months.

Mixed Fruit Wine

250 g (½ lb) each of the following fruits:

Blackberries, blackcurrants, cherries, gooseberries, plums, raspberries, redcurrants and strawberries	2 kg (4 lb) white sugar
	5 litres (1 gallon) water
	Pectic enzyme and Campden tablets
	Wine yeast

Wash, stalk, stone and crush the fruit.

Drop it as prepared into a bin containing the water, pectic enzyme and one crushed Campden tablet.

Cover and leave for 24 hours.

Stir in a quarter of the sugar and an active yeast. Ferment on the pulp for three days keeping the pulp submerged and the bin loosely covered.

Strain out and press the fruit, discard the pulp and stir in another quarter of the sugar and continue fermentation under an airlock. After one week stir in another quarter of the sugar and one week later stir in the rest.

When fermentation is finished, rack into sterilised containers and add one Campden tablet.

Store for 6–9 months before bottling. This is a splendid light red wine, fairly strong and medium sweet.

An alternative method is to liquidise the prepared fruit, strain out the solids, add the enzyme and Campden tablet to the juice and next day the sugar, water and yeast.

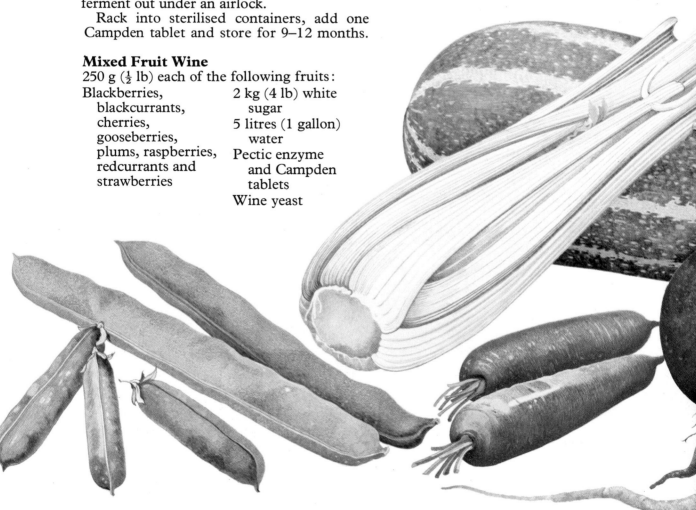

Rhubarb Wine

3 kg (6 lb) garden rhubarb
2 lemons
2 kg (4 lb) white sugar
5 litres (1 gallon) water
Pectic enzyme and Campden tablets
Wine yeast

Top and tail the rhubarb, wipe the stalks with a cloth dipped in a sulphite solution, chop them up or mince them. Thinly pare the lemons and add the rinds to the rhubarb. Pour on hot water and leave to cool.

Add the pectic enzyme, one crushed Campden tablet and the expressed juice of the lemons. Cover and leave for 24 hours.

Strain out and press the pulp dry, discard and stir in half the sugar and an active yeast and ferment under an airlock. Ten days later, stir in the rest of the sugar and continue the fermentation.

Rack the wine into sterilised containers and add one Campden tablet.

Store for 6–9 months before bottling.

Vegetable wines

Select the vegetables carefully and use only the best. Mature main crop varieties are usually the best. Scrub all root vegetables with a firm brush in clean cold water until no

trace of soil remains. Top and tail them if necessary, dice and boil them until tender. Leave them to cool, then strain off the solids, but do not press them. The wine is made only from the liquor.

Beetroot Wine

2.5 kg (5 lb) beetroot
2 lemons
5 litres (1 gallon) water
1.5 kg (3 lb) white sugar
Wine yeast

Boil the lemon rinds with the beetroot and leave to cool.

Dissolve the sugar in the liquor, add the lemon juice and an active yeast.

Ferment under an airlock.

When fermentation is finished rack into a sterilised container, add one Campden tablet and store for at least one year. When the wine is young it sometimes has an earthy taste, but this usually disappears with age.

Broad Bean Wine

1.5 kg (3 lb) shelled broad beans
2 lemons
1.5 kg (3 lb) white sugar
5 litres (1 gallon) water
Hock wine yeast

Use the broad beans from the end of the season.

Boil them with the lemon rind until tender. Dissolve the sugar in the liquor when cool, add the lemon juice and yeast.

Ferment under an airlock.

When fermentation is finished rack and add one Campden tablet.

Store for 6 to 9 months before bottling.

This is a surprisingly attractive wine.

Carrot Wine

2 kg (4 lb) prepared carrots
2 oranges and 2 lemons
2 kg (4 lb) Demerara sugar
5 litres (1 gallon) water
Wine yeast

Boil the diced carrots with the thinly pared orange and lemon rinds. When cool strain and stir in half the sugar, the fruit juice and an active yeast.

Ferment under an airlock and after 10 days stir in the rest of the sugar.

When fermentation is finished rack into a sterilised container, add one Campden tablet and store for one year.

This is a strong, sweet wine.

Celery Wine

2 kg (4 lb) prepared celery
850 g (1¾ lb) white sugar
2 oranges
2 lemons
4 litres (6 pints) water
Hock wine yeast
Campden tablets

Cut off the leaves and root stem, scrub the stalks and chop them into small pieces. Put them in a large pan with 3 litres (4½ pints) water and simmer them for half an hour. Leave to cool, then strain out and discard the celery pieces.

Boil the sugar, orange and lemon juice and the rest of the water for 20 minutes and leave to cool.

Pour the celery liquor and sugar syrup into a fermentation jar, add an activated yeast, fit an airlock and ferment the wine to dryness.

Rack into a sterilised jar, add one Campden tablet and store until bright. Siphon into bottles and keep for from 6–8 months.

Serve cold and add one saccharine tablet per bottle if this wine is too dry for you.

Marrow Wine

2.5 kg (5 lb) marrow
60 g (2 oz) root ginger
2 lemons and 2 oranges
1.5 kg (3 lb) white sugar
5 litres (1 gallon) water
Wine yeast

Wipe a large marrow with a sulphited cloth, cut it into small pieces, include the skin and seeds. Thinly pare the oranges and lemons, bruise the ginger roots and boil the marrow, rinds and ginger until the marrow is tender.

When cool, strain the liquor on to the sugar and stir well. Add the expressed juice of the oranges and lemons and an activated wine yeast. Ferment under an airlock to the end.

Rack into sterilised containers, add one Campden tablet and store for 6 months.

Without the ginger the flavour is very bland; other spices of your choice may be included, for example, cloves and cinnamon.

Parsnip Wine

1.5 kg (3 lb) prepared parsnips
2 lemons
1.5 kg (3 lb) Demerara sugar
5 litres (1 gallon) water
Madeira wine yeast

Boil the prepared parsnips with the thinly pared lemon rinds and when cool, strain on to the sugar. Stir well, add the lemon juice and active wine yeast.

Ferment under an airlock to the finish.

Rack into a sterilised container, add one Campden tablet and store for one year.

This is an old favourite, well worth making and keeping until mature.

Pea Pod Wine

2 kg (4 lb) empty pea pods
2 lemons and 2 oranges
1.5 kg (3 lb) white sugar
5 litres (1 gallon) water
Hock wine yeast

Use fresh young pea pods as soon as possible after they have been picked and shelled.

Boil them with the thinly pared orange and lemon rinds for half an hour and when cool,

Primroses, pinks (white), dandelions, elder flowers, wild roses, hawthorn, lime bracts, marigolds, bramble prunings, vine prunings

strain the liquor onto the sugar. Stir well, add the expressed orange and lemon juices and an active wine yeast.

Ferment under an airlock to the finish.

Rack into a sterilised jar, add one Campden tablet and store for 6 months.

This is a light, German-type wine that is most attractive.

Other vegetable wines

Artichokes, lettuce, mangold, runner beans, spinach, turnip and no doubt other vegetables have also been used as a base for wine. The results have been less satisfactory, however, than those from the vegetables for which recipes have been given.

The vegetables in the given recipes are sometimes blended one with another, for example, Beetroot and Parsnip.

WARNING The often quoted recipe for making 'Marrow Rum' by removing one end, scooping out the seeds and filling the space with sugar does not work and is a waste of ingredients and time.

Flower and leaf wines

It is customary to measure freshly picked flowers by volume rather than weight. Simply place the petals in a measuring jug and shake them down by gently banging the jug on a table. Do not press them down.

When dried flowers are used a 60 g (2 oz) packet is generally sufficient to flavour 5 litres (1 gallon) of wine. The packets are available from herbalists and from Home Brew shops.

Green stalks, stems, leaves and calyx boxes contain so much bitterness that every scrap must be excluded – no matter how tedious the task. Only flower heads or petals may be used.

The flowers contribute only bouquet and flavour to a wine – they contain no acid, no nutrient for the yeast and no body for the wine. All these should be added.

There are various ways of extracting the essence from the flowers. The most effective is to place the petals in a suitable vessel and to pour boiling water over them. The petals should then be rubbed vigorously against the side of the vessel with the back of a wooden spoon, a process called maceration.

When the liquor cools, citric acid and one Campden tablet should be added to protect it from infection during the period of infusion. The vessel should also be closely covered. Each day for three days the petals should be macerated and finally strained out and pressed.

Sugar is then stirred into the flower water together with an activated yeast, and fermentation is conducted under an airlock.

Many of the older recipes included sultanas and spices. Indeed, one of the popular modern ways of making flower wines is to use the flower water for the dilution of a can of concentrated grape juice and to ferment this.

Plants commonly used are Agrimony, Broom, Clover, Coltsfoot, Cowslip, Dandelion, Elderflower, Golden Rod, Gorse, Hawthorn, Lime bracts, Marigold, May Blossom, Pansy, Pinks (white), Primroses and Roses. Also Oak, Walnut leaf, Vine and Blackberry prunings.

Of them all Dandelion, Elderflower and Rose petals are, perhaps, the most popular wines, possibly because of their more ready availability. Flower wines always taste best when medium sweet rather than dry, otherwise the bouquet of the flower is contradicted by the dryness of the taste of the wine.

Dandelion Wine

2.5 litres (4 pints) dandelion heads	5 litres (1 gallon) water
2 lemons and 2 oranges	Wine yeast
1.5 kg (3 lb) white sugar	

Thinly pare the lemons and oranges, chop and peel into small pieces and macerate with the dandelion heads. Add the fruit juice and one Campden tablet when the water is cool. Three days later strain the liquor on to the sugar and stir until it is dissolved. Add an active yeast and ferment under an airlock.

Rack into a sterilised jar add one Campden tablet and keep for 6 months. If necessary sweeten the wine to taste with saccharine before bottling.

Elderflower Wine

625 ml (1 pint) elderflowers	5 litres (1 gallon) water
2 lemons	Wine yeast
1.5 kg (3 lb) white sugar	

Collect the flowers on a warm dry day when the florets are fully open. Because of their very strong perfume do not use too many flowers. Gather them from different bushes so as to mix the varieties.

Make the wine in the same way as for Dandelion Wine. Two oranges or one large grapefruit may be used instead of the lemons.

Rose Petal Wine

2.5 litres (4 pints) rose petals	5 litres (1 gallon) water
2 lemons	Wine yeast
1.5 kg (3 lb) white sugar	

Collect the petals at 'petal fall' when the rose is 'blown'. Choose petals with a strong perfume such as Josephine Bruce, Wendy Cousins, Madame Lapèrière, Fragrant Cloud, Grandmère Jenny, Super Star, etc. It is better to collect from several varieties than to make a wine from just one variety.

Make the wine in the manner already described.

Herb wines

Parsley Wine

500 g (1 lb) fresh parsley	5 litres (1 gallon) water
2 lemons	Wine yeast
1.5 kg (3 lb) white sugar	

Wash the parsley then boil it with the thinly pared lemon rind for 20 minutes.

Strain onto the sugar, stir well and when cool add the lemon juice and active yeast.

Ferment under an airlock to the finish.

Rack into sterilised containers, add one Campden tablet and store for 6 months.

Ginger Wine

100 g (3 oz) root
   ginger
250 g (8 oz) raisins
2 lemons and
   2 oranges
2 g ($\frac{1}{4}$ tsp) cayenne
   pepper

1.5 kg (3 lb) brown
   sugar
5 litres (1 gallon)
   water
Wine yeast

Bruise the root ginger with a hammer, wash and chop or liquidise the raisins, thinly pare the lemons and oranges, place them all in a bin with the cayenne pepper. Pour hot water over them and leave to cool.

Express and strain the fruit juice and add to the bin with an activated yeast. Ferment on the pulp for four days, then strain out, press and discard the solids and stir in half the sugar.

Pour the must into a jar, fit an airlock and continue the fermentation. After one week, remove half the must, stir in the rest of the sugar, return the sweetened must to the jar and the excess to a bottle alongside.

Ferment to a finish, then rack, add one Campden tablet and store for at least 6 months. Sweeten to taste if necessary before serving.

Plants to avoid

above (*top to bottom*) *Yew, laburnum, ivy, rhubarb leaves, bluebells, daffodils, buttercups, green potatoes*

opposite (*right to left, top to bottom*) *Apple mint, common mint, spearmint, parsley, camomile, thyme, dried ginger root, tea leaves*

Equipment

Whatever vessels were once forced into use by the makers of kit and country wines, the true amateur winemaker is anxious to have and use the proper equipment. Manufacturers and distributors are now supplying Home Brew shops, department stores, garden centres and chemists with a wide range of specialised equipment.

Wooden tubs and glazed crocks have given way to natural polythene bins with fitting lids. Some have grommets in the lids in which can be fitted an airlock or an immersion heater. Others have taps fitted near the base so that the contents of the bin can be easily drawn off. The bins are inert to acids, are light and easy to clean. They are fitted with handles for carrying them and usually have a graduated measure on their side. The contents can thus be easily quantified. The three most popular metric sizes are of 12, 15 and 25 litres capacity. You can get by with one, but can find use for all three. These bins are ideal of mashing fruit, fermenting on the pulp and for receiving wine from a press.

Fermentation jars can now be bought in a number of different sizes although the glass 'one gallon size' remains the most popular. Some of these actually hold 4.5 litres (8 pints),

but some hold 4.8 litres (8½ pints) and a few hold 5 litres exactly. Larger metric sizes hold 18, 25 and 27 litres equivalent to 4, 5½ and 6 gallons and are often supported in plastic frames. Polypropylene fermentation jars are available and experiments are being made with polycarbonate jars. Although transparent and unbreakable, these are at present expensive.

The narrow necks of these jars accommodate bored corks or rubber bungs in which airlocks can be fitted, as well as solid bungs. The jars can then be used both for fermentation and for storage. They have become increasingly expensive over the years and some winemakers

Assorted airlocks

A wider range of equipment

are now using a 5 litre capacity, transparent, plastic, collapsible cube fitted with an opening of the same size as the jars. These are excellent for fermentation but are not regarded as suitable for storage. Ex-wine fives, consisting of a 22.5-litre (5-gallon) polythene container in a cardboard carton may also be used for fermentation but are not recommended for long-term storage.

Glazed earthenware jars are very suitable for storage. The thick cool earthenware insulates the wine from sudden changes in temperature. The opaque texture excludes light and prevents browning from that cause. These jars are available in assorted sizes from 5–27 litres (1 to 6 gallons) but are quite heavy even when empty. Some are fitted with taps for drawing off the wine.

Polythene funnels of assorted sizes are essential. A good supply of bungs and corks, capsules, stoppers and wire cages is also needed for the different wines. Only wine bottles should be used for storage, preferably green ones. The coloured glass protects the wine from browning due to light.

A siphon need consist only of a length of plastic or rubber tubing. But most siphons have a J tube fitted at one end and a plastic tap

at the other. Other versions consist of a blocked end and a bored tube instead of a J tube. This enables the wine to be drawn across the surface of the sediment when racking and this disturbs it less. More sophisticated versions are fitted with a pump to draw up the wine.

A press and a straining bag are invaluable when making larger quantities of wine, but a straining bag is essential and a polythene strainer is often in use, too. Crushers like mangles are ideal for grapes and similar fruits and liquidisers are useful for small quantities of soft fruit. For apples a stainless steel blade on a shaft that fits on to an electric drill is very

RECORD CARD

Name or number of wine.......................................
Quantity.......... Date started............................
Base ingredients   Quantity

....
....
....
Acid ....
Pectic enzyme...
Campden tablets...
Sugar ....
Grape ....
Nutrient ....
Yeast ....
Water ....
Method ....
....
....
Specific gravity prior to fermentation..................
Specific gravity at end of fermentation.................
Probable alcohol content ....
Date racked...
Campden tablets...
Wine bright ....
Wine bottled..
Wine matured ....
Evaluation..
....
....

Example of a record card

Corks, capsules and labels

handy. A bucketful of washed, sound apples can be chopped up in seconds (see page 28). A block of oak or beech wood on the end of a broomhandle is more laborious, but quite effective. Some winemakers use a steam juice extractor. They are very effective with certain fruits, notably elderberries and the like. Failing that, a preserving pan will be useful when heat treatment of the fruit is recommended.

A thermometer is necessary for checking the temperature of the must both for heat treatment and also prior to the checking of specific gravity or the pitching in of a yeast. The hydrometer is equally essential. With its help the sugar content of a must can be controlled so that wines of a given alcohol content can be produced. A trial jar in which to check the gravity is also needed.

A bottle brush is important for cleaning bottles and jars. Different shapes and sizes can be bought for the different purposes.

A corking machine is essential for driving home cylindrical corks. One model consists of a wooden cylinder in which the corks are placed and a piston which is hit with a mallet or the like to drive the piston through the cylinder and force the softened cork into the neck of the bottle. Another model obtains the same result with a lever pressure and is quicker, easier and safer.

Casks are quite expensive but beneficial, especially for red wines. They should not be of a smaller capacity than 25 litres ($5\frac{1}{2}$ gallons) since otherwise the ratio of surface to volume is too great and the wine can become over oxidised. New casks need to be soaked to ensure that they are liquid-tight, sterilised with a strong sulphite solution and then conditioned with a spirit such as *Eau-de-Vie* or Vodka. Second hand casks need especially careful preparation and should first be filled with hot soda water to cleanse the inside before sterilising. Cider, vinegar and beer casks are not suitable and should not be used.

Whenever wine is made a careful record should be kept of the ingredients and methods used and the date of starting, fermenting, racking, storing and bottling. Jars and bottles should always be labelled. Some prepared cards may be bought but a luggage label will do equally well.

Hygiene

The single most important factor in the prevention of smells and tastes, spoiled or tainted wine is good hygiene. Our forebears used to scald vessels with boiling water and burn sulphur matches in casks. We have the aid of modern chemicals that act efficiently and with little trouble.

Stained or soiled containers can be soaked clean with the aid of Chempro SDP – a commercially used preparation. It is very effective and needs only a cool water rinse to remove any excess chlorine. There are other products marketed for cleaning and sterilising equipment but any of the kitchen cleansing products are suitable, provided it is thoroughly rinsed to remove all traces of it.

Equipment should be kept in a clean condition and sterilised with a Campden tablet and citric acid solution. Campden tablets contain sodium metabisulphite and in solution release a gas called sulphur dioxide which has toxic and inhibiting effects on fungi, moulds and bacteria. If the sulphur dioxide is reinforced with citric acid, the effect is even more pronounced. Campden tablets contain a precise amount of sulphite and so can be used with accuracy for different circumstances. Furthermore, in modest quantities sulphite stimulates the activity of wine yeasts, partly by killing or inhibiting wild yeasts, and other micro organisms. Fortunately the sulphite has no deleterious effect on the wine and is odourless and tasteless unless used in massive quantities.

Campden tablets are ideal for sterilising vessels and equipment of all kinds, for cleaning and protecting musts while pectic enzyme is working, and for adding to wine after racking to prevent oxidation and infection.

For the sterilisation of equipment, two crushed Campden tablets and half a teaspoonful of citric acid dissolved in 0.56 litres (1 pint) of cold water produce an effective solution. ALL equipment such as funnel, siphon, corks, hydrometer, etc. should be immersed in this solution before use. Bins, jars and bottles should be swirled round with it. The press should be washed over with it, the straining bag dipped in it and wrung out. The one solution may be used for all the equipment during a single session.

When fruit is in good condition, one crushed Campden tablet is sufficient to kill wild yeasts, etc. When the condition of the fruit is over-ripe or damaged two tablets should be used because there is likely to be a much larger colony of micro organisms on and in the fruit.

Wine yeast should never be added to a must containing sulphite until 24 hours has elapsed. This gives time for the sulphite to deal with the micro-organisms, to disperse and not to inhibit the wine yeast. If wine yeast is added at the same time as Campden tablets, the yeast can be killed and fermentation will not start.

At the time of racking, one Campden tablet per 5 litres (1 gallon) should always be added to the wine. This not only prevents over-oxidation with its flat, dull taste developing in the

wine caused by contact with the air, but also prevents bacteria in the wine during storage.

These few precautions, if always taken, will ensure clean, sound wine and avoid all bad flavours. Remember the three golden rules:
1. Always sterilise clean equipment with a sulphite solution before use.
2. Always wash fruit and add a crushed Campden tablet as soon as it is mashed unless hot water is being used.
3. Always add one Campden tablet per 5 litres (1 gallon) when racking wine.

Ingredients for a sterilising solution

The importance of these three simple precautions cannot be overemphasised. Problems are more easily prevented than corrected. Good hygiene prevents problems.

When a session of winemaking is finished, wash, sterilise and dry all equipment before putting it away. Mould quickly grows in damp, dark receptacles. Wipe up spilt fruit juice or wine with a sulphited cloth. Keep the outside of containers clean as well as the inside. Indeed, a clean and tidy winery is likely to be a safe one for wine. Keep equipment under cover as much as possible and always keep musts and wines well covered and well corked Attention to these simple precautions prevents waste of ingredients and effort and does more to produce sound wine than anything else.

Major and minor ingredients

You can make a palatable wine from a number of different base ingredients. Good wine can be made from fruits whether they be fresh, frozen or dried, canned, juiced or jammed. Vegetables, too, offer a good choice, and a wide range of flowers, leaves, herbs, cereals and spices can also be used to flavour wines.

Of them all, none is quite as good as the right kind of wine grape grown in a favoured position. Having stated the obvious, it must also be said that many fruit-based wines are quite as good and sometimes better than the every-day type of commercial wines. Some grapes, whether fresh, dried or concentrated added to a fruit or vegetable base improves the vinosity and character of the wine significantly. The grape possesses trace minerals, vitamins, acids and other elements that assist fermentation, bouquet, flavour and body. It is well worth-while to bear this in mind and always to include some grape in one form or another in every wine you make.

Many fruits and vegetables blend together harmoniously and, with some grape, produce a good quality wine with a complex bouquet and flavour. This is the aim of the amateur winemaker producing a wine for a purpose. It is often impossible to detect the individual ingredients used. The balance of base in-gredients is adjusted to provide bouquet, flavour, body, acidity, tannin and, of course, alcohol content. The natural sugar and acid in the fruits is taken into account so that quantities added are more precisely related to the type of wine to be produced.

The better the ingredients the better the results is a fair maxim. Over-ripe and mouldy fruit rarely produce as good a wine as the best quality fruit and vegetables, with but few exceptions, the most notable of which is bananas. For wine-making purposes, bananas are often at their best when they are black skinned, soft and over-ripe. As opportunity arises it is best to buy all such bananas as you can, so that you can peel and freeze them until required. Windfall apples can also be used successfully, as long as all the damaged, bruised or maggoty parts are first cut away so that only perfect apple remains.

Fresh fruits should otherwise always be used as quickly as possible before dehydration and diminution of flavour set in. If it is not convenient to make wine from them at that moment, wash them in a sulphite solution and freeze them until required. The freezing process helps to burst the juice cell walls and so the fruit is easier to mash when thawed. Care must be taken in the thawing process, however, to prevent oxidation or browning. Sulphiting before freezing helps. Leaving the fruit sealed until thawed also helps. Apples should be cut up and sulphited before freezing. They not only take up less room in the freezer, but the sulphite gets beneath the skin of the apples and prevents browning of the white flesh. Frozen fruits make excellent wine and a large freezer helps to spread the load of making fruit wines. It also enables you to blend fruits that ripen at different times of the year.

Dried fruits make interesting wines on their own but are often best used in combination with other ingredients. Currants, raisins and sultanas are classic examples. Dried peel is best avoided since it usually conveys a bitter taste to the wine. Dried apricots add body and subtle flavour, figs add strong flavour, dates add colour and body. Prunes are perhaps best used as a main ingredient, especially if you can get large ones. Dried elderberries, sloes and, occasionally, bilberries can be bought. They should always be washed in a sulphite/citric acid solution before use to remove the fungi, moulds and bacteria that will have settled on them. Generally speaking dehydration reduces the weight of the fruit by three-quarters and so one measure of dried fruit is approximately equal to four measures of fresh fruit.

It is customary to soak the fruit in hot water overnight to enable it to absorb the water and so dissolve its acids and sugars. The fruit must always be chopped or broken open to assist in the extraction of the goodness within.

Canned and bottled fruit juices may be used provided they have not been artificially sweetened. Manufacturers sometimes use saccharine for sweetening and this results in a sweet tasting wine. Canned and bottled fruits are usually packed in a light syrup which may be safely used.

Jams and preserves make good wine, provided the jam is pure and contains no preservative or added pectin. By its very nature jam needs a double dose of pectin-destroying enzyme. Marmalade is less successful since it is boiled with pips and pith and is often rather bitter in the finished wine.

Flowers and leaves add nothing to a wine but bouquet and flavour, but this they do most generously. A handful of dried rose petals or elderflowers may be added to a fruit must to improve its bouquet. Fruit leaves, too, may be used; for example, vine leaves and prunings can be added to gooseberries or blackcurrant leaves to apples. A few oak leaves add some tannin when this is needed.

Vegetables are fairly fully covered in the chapter 'Traditional Country Wine'. Amateur winemakers use them less. Parsnip liquor is sometimes used, however, especially with fig or orange. Carrot liquor and orange is successful and runner beans add some body to elderberry wine. The best quality vegetables are strongly recommended.

Herbs are rarely used by the amateur winemaker, nor are spices other than in mulling wines and meads. Cereals are occasionally used, notably rice with raisins, but they are mainly used as an additive. First they should be washed and cracked or crushed and they should be fermented with a cereal yeast, a strain that has an enzyme for reducing starch to some extent. Wheat is the most popular cereal to use and some experiments have been made with breakfast cereals. The results, however, cannot be compared with fruit wines, and cereals are rarely used by the serious winemakers.

Campden tablets and their use have already been described in the section on hygiene, but the importance of the tablets cannot be over-

Dried and bottled fruits, jam and fruit juice (left to right)
Dates, currants, prunes, sultanas, raisins, bottled bilberries,
strawberry jam, apricots, dried figs, grapefruit juice

emphasised and the experienced winemaker is never without them.

Pectic enzyme is another ingredient that is always used by the makers of quality wines. It is available both in liquid and powder form and contains a mixture of the two enzymes that break down the pectin in fruit and vegetables. It is marketed under a number of different trade names such as Pectolin, Pectolase, Pectozyme or Pectolytic Enzyme. The quantity to use varies slightly with the brand but instructions are always given on the label. Usually one teaspoonful per 2 kg (4 lb) fruit is sufficient. It is so helpful in the process of juice extraction and the prevention of haze that it should always be used.

Acid

Three acids are found in fruits – citric, malic and, in grapes alone, tartaric. Grapes contain all three acids other fruits contain mainly citric or mainly malic acid. When acid needs to be added to a wine, however, most winemakers add only citric acid. It is less expensive than the other two, aids fermentation and produces a good flavour. Citric acid is therefore recommended in the following recipes. The enthusiast, however, is aware of the type of acid in the fruit being used and adds the appropriate acid to make up a blend of all three. The results, although more marginal than significant, are a hallmark of the perfectionist.

Acid is essential to a wine and without it the result is bland and medicinal. Yeast will not ferment without acid and almost every wine needs some additional acid. The acid not only assists fermentation and improves the flavour of a wine, but also assists in the preservation of the wine and participates in the maturing process. Acid is the cornerstone of bouquet and flavour and should never be omitted.

Tannin is another element that in small quantities improves a wine and gives it character. Tannin is found in grape stalks, skins and pips and to some extent in pear skins, black fruits and tea leaves. Indeed, some winemakers recommend the addition of half a cup of cold tea to a must to provide the necessary tannin. Grape tannin powder can be readily bought and a level teaspoonful added to a red must and half a level teaspoonful added to a white must makes a noticeable improvement in the finished wine.

Yeast

Wine cannot be made without yeast to ferment the sugar. There are countless strains of yeast and only a few of them are suitable for making wine. Of these the best is undoubtedly the true wine yeast indigenous to the various regions where vines are grown. It is available in a number of strains developed for particular purposes. For example, champagne yeast is able to ferment under pressure and imparts distinctive bouquet and flavour to sparkling wine. Sherry yeast has a high alcohol tolerance and imparts a distinctive flavour in certain

circumstances. Sauternes yeast produces rather more glycerine than other yeasts and so helps to produce a smooth-sweet-tasting wine. It is always advantageous to use the yeast appropriate to the style of wine you wish to make.

Yeast is a tiny botanical cell, invisible to the naked eye. It reproduces itself in the presence of oxygen in a matter of three hours and will do this some thirty times or so before it dies. As soon as a cell is fully grown it begins to reproduce itself and so a very large colony is soon established. When you cut off the oxygen supply with an airlock, the yeast is forced to obtain the energy it requires to remain viable from the acid/sugar/nitrogen solution around it. In doing so it converts the sugar to alcohol and carbon dioxide. The gas comes off in the form of tiny bubbles and the alcohol remains in the solution.

To function effectively, yeast needs a slightly acid solution; a sugar solution that is not too heavy – hence the addition of sugar in several doses in the recipes – and nitrogen. This is usually available in fruits, but since they are usually diluted, additional nitrogen must be added in the form of what is called 'nutrient'. This consists of one or both of the ammonium salts – ammonium sulphate or ammonium phosphate – sometimes mixed with a little vitamin B1.

Sachets of dried yeast usually contain some nutrient salts to start the yeast working. Non-fruit wines often need an additional half to one level teaspoonful of nutrient salts per 5 litres (1 gallon). If nutrient salts are not provided with the yeast, half a teaspoonful should always be added to the must to help produce a dry wine free from off flavours.

Sugar

Sugar is the final ingredient since few base ingredients contain sufficient sugar to produce a wine that will keep well. Ordinary white household sugar is the least expensive and the most widely available. It is not immediately fermentable by yeast and must first be split into its two separate sugars, fructose and glucose. The yeast secretes an enzyme which does this, but some winemakers find it more convenient to add the sugar in a syrup form which contains the separated sugars. This is called invert sugar.

All that you have to do is to mix 1 kg (2 lb) sugar with 5 g (a level teaspoonful) citric acid in 620 ml (1 pint) water. Bring this to the boil and simmer it for 20 minutes then leave it to cool. This produces 1.25 litres (2 pints) of invert sugar syrup with a specific gravity of 1.300. It can be mixed in very easily and is immediately fermentable.

Brown sugars always add a trace of caramel to the flavour of a wine and are not recommended except for Madeira-type wines.

Ordinary drinking water from a household tap is suitable for making wine.

Preparation of the must

There are three processes in the making of wine; preparation, fermentation and maturation. In the preparation process the ingredients are assembled and prepared for fermentation, i.e. the adding of an active yeast to start converting the sugar into alcohol and carbon dioxide. Fruits, in particular, need careful attention. The preparation of flowers and vegetables have already been described.

Removing the stalks

All stalks should be removed from fruit before use as they add a bitter taste to wine. Blackcurrants and elderberries must be cleaned so that none of their tiny stalks adhere to the berries, similarly with grapes. It is better to add grape tannin powder than to leave the stalks on the fruit. Removing the stalks can be quite a tedious process, but experience shows that it is important to start with a bowl full of ripe fruit, free from stalks and unripe berries.

Washing the fruit

After removing the stalks the fruit should be washed in clean, cold, running water, to flush away the dust and many of the invisible microbes adhering to the surface. If the fruit is a little over-ripe or unsound, it is wise to give it a minute or two in a sulphite and citric acid solution before draining it.

Removing the stones

Next, the fruit should be stoned, if necessary. It is usually possible to cut the fruit in half so that the stone can be removed and discarded. The inclusion of the stone often produces a taste rather like nail varnish in the finished wine. Small pips do no harm; apple and grape pips, for example, may be left in, but care should be taken not to cut or crush them and so expose the bitter substance within them. This includes marrow and melon seeds, too.

Removing the pith

Citrous fruits must be handled with great care. The white pith is extremely bitter and can quite spoil a wine if it is included. The skin may be thinly pared with a potato peeler or rubbed off with lumps of sugar. Another method that is effective with loose skinned tangerines and the like, is to peel the fruit and then scrape away the white pith from the inside with the edge of a knife. Since only the juice of the citrous fruit is required as well as the thin skin, it is often easy to cut the husk in half and to squeeze out the juice on a pointed and fluted mould. The juice is then strained through a nylon sieve to remove the pips and pieces of pithy membrane. The pithy husk is discarded.

Crushing the fruit

Hard fruits must be crushed or cut up into small pieces. Apples and pears can be something of a problem, but a power driven crusher (see page 28) is now available to do all the hard work for you.

Soft fruits can be crushed with a potato masher or liquidised electrically.

Gooseberries and similar hard small fruit are best softened with hot water and then crushed. The berries can be crushed between your fingers or the water can be strained off temporarily while the berries are crushed with a potato masher.

Sultanas and raisins should always be washed and chopped or liquidised to release the sugar and acids within them.

Heat treatment

The extraction of the colour and goodness from elderberries, blackberries, sloes and the like can often best be achieved by heating the crushed fruit to 85°C (175°F) for a quarter of an hour. This extracts all the colour from the skins without giving the fruit a stewed taste. After the heating, leave the fruit to cool, then strain and press it. Discard the pulp and use only the juice to make the wine. Do NOT boil the fruit.

Pectic enzyme

All fruit musts should first be treated with a pectic enzyme for 24 hours to break down the pectin. One Campden tablet per 5 litres (1 gallon) should also be added to protect the must from infection and oxidation during this period. This advice is relevant whatever method of juice extraction is used. The enzyme works best in a warm environment. Too much sugar will spoil its effect.

Pulp fermentation

Those fruits that are not liquidised or juiced in one way or another are fermented on the pulp for a few days after the pectic enzyme

Removing elderberries from their stalks

treatment to extract the colour and goodness. Soaking in water leaches out the soluble constituents. The formation of a small amount of alcohol assists the water and the movement of the carbon dioxide gas increases the extraction rate. Usually cold water is used for pulp fermentation, although sometimes hot water is used to soften and break open the fruit. The fruit must be kept submerged during the fermentation to prevent the pulp floating above the water and juice where it might dry out and become a source of infection from potentially harmful organisms. Also, if the fruit is not in

Always wash fruit well

the water, the goodness cannot be extracted from it. It is best to keep the fruit submerged with a platen of non-resinous wood with some holes drilled through it to allow the gas to escape. A china plate is also effective since the gas can escape from under the lip of the plate. Otherwise, the fruit cap must be pressed down twice a day and turned over. The bin must be kept covered, but not so tightly that gas cannot escape.

Balancing the must body
Before the yeast is added consideration must be given to the balance of the must. The right amount of fruit of different kinds must be included to provide sufficient body and flavour. Bananas are of great advantage in this respect. Dried apricots, too, are beneficial. Some acid fruit should be included if available, particularly a few cooking apples rich in malic acid. This provides a fruity freshness in the bouquet and flavour. Don't forget to include some concentrated grape juice, sultanas, raisins, fresh grapes or even vine leaves and prunings to add vinosity.

Acid
There must always be an adequate amount of acid present and if there is insufficient natural acid then some acid crystals should be added

All fruit must should first be treated with a pectic enzyme for 24 hours

Heat treatment of gooseberries

at the outset. Acid testing papers are available and whilst they are not very precise, they do give an indication whether the acidity of the liquid being tested is low, medium or high. Some fruits like bananas, dates and figs are deficient in acid. Others like blackcurrants and rhubarb are high and have some to spare for other fruits.

Table wines of modest alcohol content need a medium acidity. Strong, sweet wines need a higher acidity to balance the extra alcohol and sugar.

Tannin

Tannin must also be considered. Mostly it is lacking and some grape tannin powder should be added appropriate to the ingredients used and the type of wine being made.

Water

If the fruit has been liquidised or juiced, the total quantity of must should be made up with cold tap water or cold boiled water. Just how much to add is a matter of convenience. Country winemakers tend to use 5 litres (1 gallon) of water. When the juice from the fruit and the space occupied by the sugar is taken into account up to 8 bottles of wine are usually made rather than 6. This ensures that there is always plenty of extra wine of

The Pulpmaster apple crusher. Use with great care because of the speed with which the blades revolve

the same kind to use in topping up jars to keep them full.

The amateur, on the other hand, tends to use more precise quantities, and with greater skill in siphoning the wine from its sediment, loses very little wine and so needs less for topping up. In any case there is likely to be some other wine available that can be used even if it is not precisely the same. The recipes in this section are calculated to produce 6 bottles of wine, although in the first instance there may be half a bottle of must in excess to be fermented alongside the main jar (see page 33).

The amount of water to add, then, depends on which method you wish to follow, but

Pressing apple pulp

allowance must be made for the sugar or the sugar syrup, otherwise the wine will be out of balance.

Sugar

Finally the sugar content must be checked so that you can calculate how much extra sugar is needed.

Having diluted the fruit juice appropriately check the specific gravity with a hydrometer and record its reading. This indicates the natural sugar content of the must.

If the must is to be fermented on the pulp, give it a good stir 24 hours after adding the pectic enzyme and just prior to adding the

yeast. Remove a jugful of pulp and juice and strain it through a nylon sieve or straining bag. Squeeze the pulp dry, measure the specific gravity of the extract and record this reading. Return the juice and pulp to the bulk of the must. You can now calculate from the tables in the next chapter (see page 31) how much sugar you will need to add.

Records

If you have not already done so, this is a good time to fill in a record card with the name of the wine and details of the ingredients and quantities used and the date. During a season of winemaking when a number of different wines are made it is essential to keep a record of each wine. It is otherwise impossible to remember whether this or that has been done to a particular wine, when it is due for racking, how strong it is, etc. Having taken trouble in the preparation of a wine it is foolish not to keep an adequate record. Experience shows time and time again how useful the record can be.

Preparing the yeast

When the must has been prepared and the pectic enzyme added, the bin covered and put away for 24 hours, a yeast starter should be prepared. Yeast is usually sold as tiny dry granules, as a compressed tablet or as a thin, putty-coloured liquid. In all cases it is in a dormant state and needs to be re-activated before use. Many winemakers have their own formulae for doing this. Some use a weak malt extract solution, others use some of the must itself. One simple and effective method is to use a dessertspoonful of concentrated grape juice dissolved in a tumbler of cold boiled water. This contains sufficient acid, nutrient, sugar, vitamins and minerals to get the yeast started. It should be poured into a sterilised bottle leaving plenty of head space to provide oxygen for the developing cells. The yeast is then added, the neck loosely plugged with cotton wool and the bottle left in a warm place, say, 24°C (75°F). Every now and then give the bottle a shake to stimulate the take up of oxygen and within 6 to 12 hours you should see bubbles rising in the solution. Sometimes, and more frequently with tablets of compressed yeast than with loose granules, re-activation might take 24 or even 48 hours.

When the yeast is fermenting effectively and added to the must you can be sure that fermentation will soon begin. Whether all liquid, or containing some fruit pulp, give the must a good stir so that it can take up some more oxygen from the air. Loosely cover a pulp must and fit an airlock to a liquid must. Leave some air space in case of frothing when fermentation begins.

Fermentation of the must

Without alcohol, wine would be nothing more than a diluted, sweet fruit juice. Alcohol is formed from the sugar by the action of the enzymes secreted by the yeast cells. The control of the sugar content of the must is therefore of considerable importance. For practical purposes, the quantity of sugar in a must is measured by a hydrometer. Usually the liquid to be tested is poured into a trial jar containing the hydrometer. When the instrument is floating and still, a note is made of the figure level with the surface of the liquid.

Specific gravity

In ordinary water at 15°C (59°F) this reading is 1.000. When sugar and/or some other dissolved solids are present, the figure will be higher. This indicates that the weight or gravity of the liquid is greater than the weight or gravity of the water. Reference is made to the specific gravity of a liquid because the gravity of the liquid being tested is specifically related to the gravity of the same volume of water.

By reference to the tables that follow it will be seen that the different specific gravity figures represent different weights of sugar dissolved in 5 litres (1 gallon) of the liquid.

How much alcohol?

It is known that almost half (about 47.5% to be more accurate) of the sugar can be converted by yeast into alcohol. About the same quantity becomes carbon dioxide gas and the remaining 5% becomes glycerine, wine acids, etc. During the conversion some heat is generated and this raises the temperature of the must slightly.

By measuring the weight or gravity of the sugar in the must and by adding to it only enough sugar to increase that gravity sufficiently to produce as much alcohol as is required for the type of wine being made, we can control the alcohol content of our wines fairly well. The figures are not absolutely

A thermal pad and a thermal belt

precise because of the presence of a small but unknown quantity of dissolved solids in the must. Furthermore, alcohol is lighter in weight than water and as it is formed it dilutes the water to some extent. Nevertheless, for all practical purposes the figures represent a fair approximation for our needs.

The specific gravity figures in the table are taken at a temperature of 15°C (59°F). If the temperature of the liquid is higher, some adjustment must be made to the last figure of the specific gravity reading.

For example:

Temperature of liquid	Addition to last figure
20°C (68°F)	0.9
25°C (77°F)	2.0
30°C (86°F)	3.4
35°C (95°F)	5.0
40°C (104°F)	6.8

By using the hydrometer we can find out how much sugar is in the must and we can calculate how much extra sugar is needed. By

Conversion tables

Specific gravity	Sugar in 1 gallon	5 litres	Approx. probable % volume of alcohol *after* fermentation
	oz	gram	
1.005	2¾	85	
1.010	4¾	150	0.4
1.015	7	220	1.2
1.020	9	285	2.0
1.025	11	350	2.8
1.030	13¼	415	3.6
1.035	15½	485	4.3
1.040	17½	550	5.1
1.045	19½	615	5.8
1.050	21½	680	6.5
1.055	23¾	745	7.2
1.060	25¾	810	7.9
1.065	27¾	875	8.6
1.070	30	945	9.3
1.075	32	1010	10.0
1.080	34½	1075	10.6
1.085	36½	1140	11.3
1.090	38½	1205	12.0
1.095	40¾	1275	12.7
1.100	42¾	1340	13.4
1.105	44¾	1405	14.2
1.110	47	1475	14.9
1.115	49	1540	15.6
1.120	51¼	1605	16.3
1.125	53¼	1675	17.1
1.130	55½	1740	17.8

Note 1 kg sugar increases the volume of a liquid by 0.62 litre. 2 lb sugar increases the volume of a liquid by 1 pint.

An activated yeast

taking regular readings we can also follow the progress of a fermentation.

Stuck ferments

If fermentation should stop prematurely, something may have gone wrong. For example:
1. If there is insufficient acid or nutrient in the must the yeast will not be able to continue functioning. Reference to your record card will remind you of what was included and whether lack of acid or nutrient is likely to be the cause. If it is, stir in some citric acid and nutrient.
2. The must might have become too hot or too cold and has inhibited the yeast function. The ideal temperature for white wines is 16°C (61°F) and for red wines 20°C (68°F), but yeast will normally ferment between 10°C (50°F) and 30°C (86°F). Check the temperature and if it is too cool or too hot, move the must to a different position with the appropriate temperature.

3. The yeast colony may have become weak or inhibited by dissolved carbon dioxide. The remedy is to pour the must from one container to another in such a rough manner that carbon dioxide is pushed out and oxygen is absorbed. Repeat this process two or three times only.

4. Possibly the alcohol tolerance of the yeast has been reached. Reference to your record card will remind you of the original gravity and the amount of sugar added. All wine yeasts can ferment up to 12% alcohol, but if this figure is exceeded it may be a cause for fermentation to cease.

5. If fermentation stops soon after starting it may be that there is so much sugar in the must that the syrup is too heavy for the yeast to ferment and it has died in the attempt. Your record card will again remind you of the original gravity. Experience shows that fermentation is best when the initial specific gravity is not too high. It is better to calculate the total amount of sugar required and to add this in three or four doses rather than all together in one dose. Never exceed 1.090 as a starting gravity. If too much sugar is the problem, make up another must without sugar and mix the two together. This will reduce the sugar to a level at which a new and active yeast can ferment.

6. If all tests prove negative – if you have satisfied yourself that there is nothing wrong with the temperature, that the must contained sufficient acid and nutrient and not too much sugar, and that all the sugar has not been fermented – and if you have aerated the must and still it will not ferment, then make up another yeast starter.

Re-starting the ferment

Do not add the activated yeast to the stuck must, however, but slowly add the must to the yeast. Double the quantity each time you add some must, but do not add the next lot until the last lot is fermenting. Start by adding an equal quantity of must to the starter and when that is working add another equal quantity and so on until all the must is working again.

A good fermentation is obtained from an

Preparing a yeast starter

active yeast colony in a must rich in acid and nutrient, not too heavy in sugar and situated in an even temperature. Wide fluctuations in temperature rising to the near maximum during the day, yet falling to just above freezing at night puts a strain on the yeast cells which they cannot tolerate.

Keeping it warm

If you have to ferment your musts in an un-heated room in winter, then use an immersion heater in the must, or a thermal belt around the jar, or stand the jar on a thermal pad (see page 30). Wrap the jars up in insulating material if these facilities are not available.

These conditions are particularly important when you wish to make a strong wine. The sugar must be added in small doses as indicated by the reducing specific gravity. Never let the gravity rise very high and add a little more sugar as the gravity falls to near zero. Keep a note of the number of units fermented between each addition of sugar from the very outset, and add them up at the end of fermentation so that you can see from the conversion tables approximately how much alcohol the wine contains.

Sweet wines

Strong wines can be fermented to the very limit of the alcohol tolerance of the yeast and after racking they can be sweetened to suit your palate. Sweet table wines of lower alcohol content can be made by terminating the fermentation at an appropriate point. A sweet table wine needs 11 to 12% alcohol and a residual sweetness equivalent to a specific gravity of between 1.016 and 1.026, depending on your palate and the wine.

When a sufficient quantity of alcohol has been formed, rack the wine into a sterilised jar, sweeten it to suit your palate and add one Campden tablet containing sodium meta-bisulphite and one Vingard tablet containing potassium sorbate to each 5 litres (1 gallon) of wine. These two tablets will prevent re-fermentation and will ensure that the wine remains stable. Either tablet is insufficient on its own. As soon as the wine is bright, rack it again but further tablets are not necessary.

When fermentation finishes, the specific gravity of a dry wine should be between 0.998 and 0.990. Medium and sweet wines can be terminated as just described at any specific gravity you wish. There is much to be said for fermenting all wines out to dryness, attaining the alcohol content of your choice. When the wine has been clarified it can be sweetened to suit your palate, treated with the two tablets just mentioned and left for a while longer to mature.

An elderberry dessert wine ready for fermentation. Note the headroom in the jar to allow for the addition of sugar and the excess in the bottle for topping up

Hydrometer at specific gravity 10.80

Maturing the young wines

As soon as fermentation finishes and the young wine is racked from its sediment the process of maturation begins. This may take from a couple of months to several years before the wine is just right for drinking. At times in between it may smell and taste unpleasant, but provided the wine is clean and sound, these features will disappear and eventually the wine will taste smooth and enjoyable.

The process of racking – removing the clear wine from its sediment – is as old as wine-making itself. It has long been regarded as something of a panacea or treatment for all ailments. Wines that are slow to clear often benefit by being racked into a sterilised container with a Campden tablet. Within a few days a further deposit can often be seen.

During maturation further chemical changes and reactions go on in the wine. These are best carried out slowly and so wine should be stored at an even temperature, between 10°C (50°F) and 12°C (54°F). The wine does not suffer if it is slowly reduced to an even lower temperature for a while. Indeed, this assists not only with the clarification of the wine but also with the precipitation of cream of tartar crystals from the reaction of potassium salts with tartaric acid.

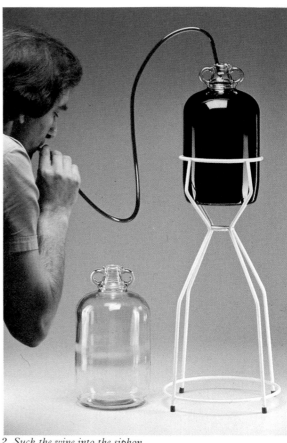

2. Suck the wine into the siphon

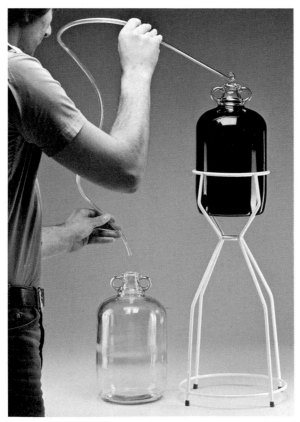

1. Insert the siphon into the full jar

3. Cover the end of the siphon with your finger and place that end in the empty jar

Finings

Most wines clear naturally by themselves. Some achieve clarity even before fermentation is finished, some take several months to clear. If clarity is required quickly, or if a wine is stubborn to clear, the wine may be fined with some proprietary finings. These usually consist of a mixture of an isinglass gel, citric acid and sulphite, that must be diluted and stirred into the wine. Another fining agent consists of a bentonite gel that is used in the same way. Sometimes a combination of gelatine and tannin is also used. Another fining agent is the white only of an egg beaten into some wine and stirred into the bulk, but one egg is enough for 25 litres (5 gallons). Fresh milk is sometimes effective too – especially with apples wines. One or two tablespoonsful per 5 litres (1 gallon) is usually enough.

After stirring finings into a wine, it must be left in a cool place for a few days while the fining agent coagulates the suspended solids and sinks with them to the bottom of the container. As soon as the wine is bright it should be racked again. The suspended solids often include dead yeast cells and fruit or vegetable pulp. If this matter is not removed from the wine it will decompose and taint the wine with a revolting smell and taste.

It is unwise to rack an actively fermenting wine in which a deposit can be seen, because this often stops the fermentation. The deposit should be removed as soon as the fermentation stops naturally and again whenever it is noticed during the period of maturation. Three or four rackings are not too many.

Racking is best done with a siphon and, provided the receiving vessel is beneath the vessel to be racked, gravity will slowly draw the wine from one vessel to the other.

Filtering

Filtering is very rarely necessary and should be looked upon as a last resort. Although they have been considerably improved, filters for use in the home are nowhere near as good as those used in commerce. All too often the wine trickles through so slowly that it is at risk both from infection and over-oxidation. Filtering also removes tannin as well as the suspended fine particles and can leave a wine poorer than it was. Worse still, the filtering agent sometimes leaves a cardboardy taste in the wine.

Special hazes

Before rushing into filtering it is better to discover just what is the cause of the offending haze. If it does not respond to fining with a

4. Gravity will transfer the wine from the jar above to the jar below

5. Siphoning finished. Discard the sediment in the jar above. Top up the jar below

proprietary agent, the haze may be due to pectin. This can be discovered by mixing a teaspoonfull of wine with a tablespoonful of methylated spirits, shaking it up well and leaving it for half an hour or so. If the cause of the haze is pectin, strings or clots will appear in the methylated spirits. A pectolytic enzyme should be dissolved in the wine, which should be transferred to a warm place for a few days to encourage the breakdown of the pectin. As the wine clears, a deposit will form and the wine should be racked.

Occasionally a starch haze will form, especially from vegetable and cereal musts. The presence of starch can be ascertained by adding a few drops of tincture of iodine to a tablespoonful of wine in a saucer. If the wine darkens or changes colour towards blue, then starch is present. The remedy is to mix in some fungal amylase to dissolve the starch. The quantity to use is given on the packet. Sometimes a clear wine will suddenly become hazy again. This is nearly always due to a bacterial infection. It could have been prevented by the addition of a Campden tablet when the wine was racked. Add two crushed Campden tablets per 5 litres (1 gallon) and rack the wine again when it clears.

Unsulphited wine may also develop a shiny, oily appearance and this too is due to a bacterial infection. Pour the wine into a bin, beat it well to break up the chains of bacteria and add two crushed Campden tablets. Pour the wine back into a sterilised jar and a few days later rack it from the deposit.

Fortunately these infections are few and far between. They can always be prevented by the wise use of Campden tablets.

Bulk storage
Wines develop better in bulk than in bottle because the chemical reactions are on a larger scale. Most white wines benefit from some months in bulk storage before bottling. Red wines benefit from a year or two. Indeed, robust red wines benefit from a year in cask, provided the cask is large enough and kept full to the bung.

All storage vessels must be kept full to the bung and tightly sealed otherwise the wine will become infected with a fungus called 'flowers of wine'. This is a creamy coloured powder that forms on the surface of wine in the presence of air. If left long enough it will reduce the alcohol in the wine to water. Should you notice this infection in a vessel, remove the loose cork and fill the container carefully, drop by drop, with similar wine or cold boiled water, until the fungus is floated off. Add a crushed Campden tablet and seal the vessel tightly.

Bottling
When bottling time comes, first check that the wine is quite dry and has been sulphited or if it is sweet, has been treated with sorbate and sulphite. Wash and sterilise all the wine bottles to be filled and drain them. Siphon the wine into the bottles to within 2 cm ($\frac{3}{4}$ in) of the bottom of the cork. Soften the clylindrical corks by soaking them, well submerged in a sulphite solution for several hours, fit them one at a time into a corking tool and ram the cork home flush.

Fit a plastic or foil cover over the mouth and neck of the bottle and stick, or tie on a label. Lay the bottle on its side in a wine rack or in a cardboard wine carton placed in an evenly cool position throughout the year. A few more months and the wine will be ready for drinking. Bottle age is important for your best wines and well worth the extra period of waiting. It may prove helpful to bottle some of the wine in half size bottles so that these can be tasted first and the progress of the wine monitored.

Blending
Sadly, not every wine turns out to be a 'crackerjack' any more than commercial wines. This fact is usually revealed when you are about to bottle the wine. Out of ten wines, three may be very good, six may be average and one may be disappointing. There may be nothing more wrong with this last wine than a poor flavour due to poor fruit. Do not despair, however, there is a simple remedy.

Provided the wines are clean and sound and free from infection of every kind, they can be blended together. The result is almost always a greatly improved wine infinitely superior to the wines that went into it. Blending wines is something of an art. If some gardeners have green fingers, some wine makers certainly have a purple thumb, especially when it comes to blending.

First taste the wines that you are thinking of blending and assess their virtues and defects. Pour into a large glass jug a measure of each wine, stir gently and taste. It may be necessary to add an extra half or whole measure or more of certain wines until you achieve a blend to your liking. Now mix the wines in the proportion worked out in the jug, stir gently and put the blend into clean, sterilised containers. Add one Campden tablet per gallon and fit airlocks to the containers. Some fermentation may take place, there will certainly be some chemical reactions and a deposit may be thrown.

After a month or two the wine should be ready for drinking. If it is an everyday wine, it may be best to rack it into a *Wine Maid* and serve it direct from that container into a carafe for the table.

Doctoring

If you have too few wines to blend you can sometimes improve a wine with a little more acid or tannin or flavouring or sweetening. One saccharine tablet per bottle works wonders in taking the rough edge off a too dry wine or masking some poor flavour. It is quite exceptional to make a wine that is so unpalatable as not to be worth drinking. If you have failed to rack the wine adequately or to sulphite against infection you have only yourself to blame. If the wine is otherwise clean and sound it can always be improved. Indeed, the French wine trade make a range of wines called 'vins medecins' solely for 'doctoring' or improving wines deficient in some quality.

The great majority of all the commercial wines that are sold are a blend of different wines. Amateur winemakers seem to think that they lose face if they admit to blending their average wines. In point of fact, many wines would be greatly improved and reputations also, if the art of blending was practised a good deal more.

Before drinking your wines, then, consider them objectively, assess them critically and have the courage to improve them by blending. You can then devise a fancy name for the blend and so extend your pleasure in serving well balanced wine of good flavour.

Wines after their first racking and ready for storage until bright, when they must be racked again

Table wines

Introduction

Tables wines are those that are especially suitable for drinking with meals. They may be red, white or rosé. The red wines are always dry, that is, lacking any taste of sweetness. The white wines may be either dry for drinking with main course dishes, such as fish, poultry or pork, or sweet, for drinking with the sweet or dessert course. Rosé wines are usually just dry or medium dry and are particularly suitable for drinking with buffet or picnic meals.

Because the wines are served with food, it is customary to drink several glasses of them during a meal. For this reason, then, the alcohol content of table wines should be kept to a modest level and from 10 to 12% is considered to be strong enough.

This level of alcohol is achieved by controlling the total quantity of sugar used, ensuring that the yeast has sufficient acid and nutrient and that the fermentation temperature is kept reasonably constant at around 20°C (68°F).

The flavour of table wines should be subtle, complex and vinous, rather than redolent of the flavour of a single ingredient. Most grape wines are made from a mixture of different grape varieties, selected for their contribution to the colour, acidity, sweetness, etc. It seems only sensible that amateur winemakers should take notice of this approach and a blend of ingredients is therefore recommended in the recipes that follow, in order to achieve a satisfactory balance.

The best quality ingredients make the best wine, although good wine can also be made from fallen or damaged fruit, provided the bruised or damaged portions are cut out and discarded. Before use, the fruit should be cleaned from its stalks, large stones should be removed, the fruit should be washed free from dust, crushed and treated with sulphite. This prevents oxidation (browning), kills off many of the wild fungi and bacteria and inhibits the growth of the remainder. It also affects wine yeasts to some extent and so a wine yeast culture should never be added to a must until 24 hours *after* the sulphite.

A pectin-destroying enzyme should also be added in accordance with the manufacturer's instructions. This ensures a better juice extraction and prevents pectin haze in the finished wine.

Most fruit wines are made by the process of pulp fermentation, especially when large quantities of fruit are being used. The developing alcohol and the bubbling gas assists in the leaching out of all the soluble substances in the fruit. Soft fruits may be liquidised and fermented in a narrow-necked jar fitted with an airlock.

Fresh fruits should never be boiled since this impairs the flavour of the finished wine. When colour is to be extracted, the crushed fruit may be heated to 80°C (175°F) and kept at this temperature for about fifteen minutes. The fruit should then be cooled, strained and pressed. The dry pulp is discarded and only the juice is used.

Vegetables should be topped, tailed, thoroughly cleaned from all trace of soil, chopped into small pieces and gently boiled until tender. The liquor is strained off, cooled and used for the wine.

In the recipes that follow, quantities are given in metric and Imperial measures for making 5 litres or one gallon of wine. Use either the metric or Imperial quantities but not a mixture of each for the same wine. The precise quantities of the major ingredients are not critical because of the wide variations in their quality due to the different varieties of the same fruit, the location in which they were grown and the weather of the season. The juiciness or otherwise of the fruit can also marginally affect the precise amount of water used. All the quantities mentioned should be increased pro rata to make larger quantities of wine, but one sachet of yeast is sufficient to ferment from 5–27 litres (1–6 gallons) of wine.

The first recipe is given in greater detail than the others to familiarize you with the technique and to avoid too much repetition.

Apple Wine

Many experienced amateur winemakers agree that apples and combinations of apples with other fruits make some of our best wines. A good mixture of apples is often freely or cheaply available and you are strongly recommended to make apple based wines in large quantities.

4 kg (8 lb) mixed eating and cooking apples	5 g (1 tsp) citric acid
	2 g ($\frac{1}{2}$ tsp) grape tannin
250g ($\frac{1}{2}$ lb) sultanas or concentrated white grape juice	Pectic enzyme and Campden tablets
750 g (1$\frac{1}{2}$ lb) approximately, white sugar	2.5 litres (4$\frac{1}{2}$ pints) cold water
	Champagne wine yeast and nutrient

1. Pour the water into a sterilised polythene bin and mix in the acid, pectic enzyme and one crushed Campden tablet.
2. Wash the apples free from dust and crush

them or cut them into small pieces. Drop them at once into the water in the bin.

Cover the bin and leave it in a warm place 21°C (70°F) for 24 hours while the pectin is destroyed.

3. and 4. Wash and chop the sultanas and add to the bin or pour in the concentrated grape juice. Any unused concentrate can be covered and stored in the refrigerator for months.

Add an activated wine yeast (see page 29) with nutrient and tannin.

Replace the cover and leave for 24 hours in the same warm place.

5. Stir the pulp, remove a jugful, strain it through a nylon bag and press the pulp.

6. Pour this juice into a hydrometer trial jar, insert the hydrometer and when it is floating steady, note the reading and record it. The specific gravity will probably be in the region of 1.030, depending on the sweetness of the fruit, but it may be higher or a little lower.

Return the juice and pulp to the bin, replace the cover and leave the fruit to ferment for another five or six days.

7. Press down the floating fruit into the juice twice each day or, better still, keep it submerged with the aid of a china plate. (See overleaf).

8. Strain out and press the fruit dry in a small press or with your hands. Frequently stir up the pulp in the bag to ensure the maximum juice extraction.

Check the specific gravity again and stir in sufficient sugar to bring the total gravity reading up to 1.085. For example, if the original reading was 1.030 and the present reading is 1.002, then you need to add sufficient sugar to increase the present reading from 1.002 to 1.057. (1.030 − 1.002 = 28 units already fermented. 1.085 − 28 = 1.057). It will be seen by reference to the tables on page 31 that a reading of 1.057 is the approximate equivalent of 750 g (1½ lb) sugar. If the apples are sweeter and the original reading is higher than 1.030, then slightly less sugar will be required. If the reading is lower than 1.030, then more sugar will be required.

9. Pour the must into a sterilised fermentation jar, top up with cold boiled water if necessary, and fit an airlock. If there is a small excess of must, pour this into a sterilised bottle that will just contain it and plug the neck with cotton wool.

Continue the fermentation in the same warm place until the wine is still and begins to clear from the neck downwards, then move the jar to a cooler place for a few days to assist the clearing process. In the absence of thermal currents in the wine caused by the warmth, the sediment settles more quickly.

10. Siphon the clearing wine into a sterilised jar, top up with the excess wine from the bottle, or with some similar wine, or with cold boiled water, or with sterilised marbles or pebbles. In any event, fill the jar and add one Campden tablet to prevent oxidation and infection of the wine from bacteria.

11. Bung the jar tight, label and store it in a cool place for from 6 to 8 weeks. If a further

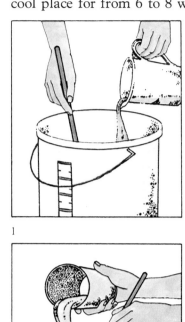
1

2

3

4

5

6

1. Water, acid, enzyme and sulphite in bin
2. Add the apples immediately after cutting
3. Add grape juice OR
4. Add chopped sultanas
5. Remove some pulp and juice
6. Check specific gravity with hydrometer

deposit has been thrown, siphon the wine into another sterilised jar, top it up as before and store for a further 6 to 8 months.

If the wine is still hazy, fine it with some proprietary finings in accordance with the manufacturer's instructions or with two table-spoonfuls of fresh milk, well stirred into the wine. Left in the coldest place available, the wine should be clear within a week and then racked from its sediment.

12. When the wine is around 9 months old. siphon it into sterilised bottles, fit sterilised and softened corks, label and store for a further 3 to 6 months.

Serve this wine nicely chilled with appropriate food for white wine, but especially with roast pork.

NOTE Step 8. may be omitted if you do not have a hydrometer. The quantity of sugar recommended in this and the other recipes will be found to be adequate.

Variations
1. A *Medium Sweet Apple Wine* can be made by dissolving one or two crushed saccharine tablets in each bottle of wine just prior to serving.

2. A *Sweet Apple Wine* can be made by increasing the quantity of apples by 500 g (1 lb), the sultanas or grape concentrate by 125 g ($\frac{1}{4}$ lb) and the sugar by 250 g ($\frac{1}{2}$ lb). Two level teaspoonfuls of citric acid will be required instead of one.

If you use a hydrometer, the total gravity should be increased to 105 and fermentation should be stopped at 1.015 by racking the still fermenting wine from its sediment into a sterilised jar containing one gram of potassium sorbate and one crushed Campden tablet. This will stop the fermentation by killing all the yeast cells. Leave the jar of wine in a cool place for a few days, then rack again and store.

Without a hydrometer it is more difficult to know just when to terminate fermentation, but after the wine has been in the jar for about 2 weeks fermentation should be stopped.

3. *Sparkling Apple Wine* can be made by re-fermenting a bright and dry apple wine when it is 6 months old. Follow the detailed instructions given on pages 56–59.

4. *Orchard Wine* is made by using fewer apples in the basic recipe and replacing them with 1 kg (2 lb) hard pears, 500 g (1 lb) crab apples, such as John Downie or Yellow Siberian, and 250 g ($\frac{1}{2}$ lb) small Japanese quince. The latter have a beautiful perfume which they convey both in bouquet and flavour to the finished wine.

5. *Bottled or canned apple juice* may be used instead of fresh apples. Empty a quart can of apple juice into a sterilised fermentation jar, add the concentrated white grape juice, the sugar dissolved in warm water and cooled, the acid, tannin, active yeast and nutrient from the basic recipe. Top up with cold boiled water, fit an airlock and continue as already described.

6. Concentrated apple juice for use instead of fresh apples is available in some Home Brew shops. It is made up in the same way as con-

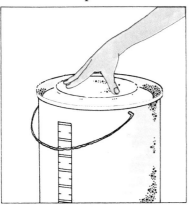
7

8

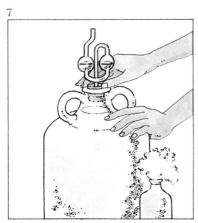
9

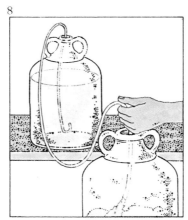
10

11

12

7. *Return pulp and press down*
8. *Press juice from apple pulp*
9. *Fit an airlock*
10. *Rack the young wine from its sediment*
11. *Bung tight, label and store*
12. *Bottle and cork the wine*

centrated grape juice and full instructions are given with each pack.

7. Apples and other fruits also blend together to make good wines. To the basic recipe add 1 kg (2 lb) blackberries, or 1 kg (2 lb) damsons, or 500 g (1 lb) elderberries, or 1 kg (2 lb) gooseberries, or 1 kg (2 lb) plums – any variety – or 500 g (1 lb) raspberries, or almost any other kind of fruit available to you. Use black grape juice concentrate with the black fruits to produce red wines.

Apricot Wine

Fresh, dried and canned apricots all make good wines on their own and blend well with other fruits.

2 kg (4 lb) fresh apricots	2 g ($\frac{1}{2}$ tsp) grape tannin
2 ripe bananas	Pectic enzyme and Campden tablets
$\frac{1}{2}$ lb sultanas	
1 kg (2 lb) white sugar	3 litres (5 pints) water
10 g (2 tsp) citric acid	Burgundy wine yeast and nutrient

Dissolve the acid, pectic enzyme and one crushed Campden tablet in the water.

Remove stalks, wash, stone and crush the apricots or liquidise both the apricots and the sultanas, together with the peeled bananas.

Add all the fruit to the water, cover and leave for 24 hours.

Stir in an activated yeast nutrient and tannin. Ferment on the pulp for three days keeping it submerged.

Strain out the pulp, discard, stir in the sugar, pour the must into a jar, fit an airlock and ferment to dryness.

Rack into a sterilised storage jar and add one Campden tablet.

When the wine is bright, rack again and store for 6 months before bottling. Keep the wine for another 3 months at least. It is very good with poached fish and smoked haddock.

Dried Apricot, Banana and Rhubarb Wine

375 g ($\frac{3}{4}$ lb) dried apricots	2 g ($\frac{1}{2}$ tsp) grape tannin
2 ripe bananas	Pectic enzyme and Campden tablets
1 kg (2 lb) garden rhubarb	
250 g ($\frac{1}{2}$ lb) sultanas	4 litres (7 pints) water
1 kg (2 lb) white sugar	Burgundy wine yeast and nutrient
5 g (1 tsp) citric acid	

Wash the apricots, cut them up into small pieces and soak them in hot water overnight.

Next day peel the bananas, slice them thinly, add them to the apricots and heat them in the water in which the apricots have been soaking for fifteen minutes at 80°C (175°F). Leave them to cool.

Top and tail the rhubarb, wipe the stalks with a cloth soaked in a sulphite solution, cut them up into small pieces, put them into a bin containing the rest of the water, the acid, pectic enzyme and one crushed Campden tablet. Add the apricots, bananas and juice. Cover and leave for 24 hours.

Add an activated yeast, nutrient and tannin and ferment on the pulp for 3 days keeping the fruit submerged.

Strain out the fruit, discard the pulp, stir in the sugar, pour the must into a jar, fit an airlock and continue fermentation to dryness.

Rack the clearing wine, add one Campden tablet and store until bright. Rack again and keep for 6 months before bottling, then store for a few months longer. Serve chilled with any white wine dish.

Canned Apricot, Gooseberry and Plum Wine

1 can each apricots, gooseberries and golden plums (approx. 450 g/ 1 lb)	10 g (2 tsp) citric acid
	2 g ($\frac{1}{2}$ tsp) grape tannin
250 g ($\frac{1}{4}$ can) concentrated white grape juice	Pectic enzyme and Campden tablets
800 g (1$\frac{3}{4}$ lb) white sugar	3 litres (5 pints) water
	Burgundy wine yeast and nutrient

Open each can of fruit and strain the syrup into a sterilised bottle, seal it and store it in the refrigerator until required.

Mash or liquidise the fruit and stir it into the water containing one crushed Campden tablet, the acid and the pectic enzyme. Cover and leave for 24 hours.

Stir in the syrup, concentrated grape juice, activated yeast, nutrient and tannin. Ferment on the pulp for 3 days keeping the fruit submerged.

Strain out the pulp, roll it round a nylon bag or sieve, but do not squeeze it. Discard pulp.

Stir in the sugar, pour the must into a fermentation jar, fit an airlock and ferment to dryness.

Rack the clearing wine, add one Campden tablet and store until bright. Rack straight into sterilised bottles and keep the wine until it is about 3–4 months old. Serve it nicely chilled as a wine aperitif or with light food. It is particularly refreshing on a hot day.

Apricot Nectar

Use one large bottle of apricot nectar instead of the canned fruit in the recipe above.

Bilberry Wine

Bilberries are small, currant-like berries and are grown in many gardens. Some people call them blueberries or whortleberries. They can also be bought bottled or canned in syrup. They make excellent red wine by themselves and blend very well with blackberries, blackcurrants, damsons, elderberries and sloes, so improving the colour, bouquet and flavour.

1 kg (2 lb) approx. bilberries in syrup	4 g (1 tsp) grape tannin
250 g (½ lb) concentrated black grape juice	Pectic enzyme and Campden tablets
1 kg (2 lb) white sugar	3 litres (5 pints) water
10 g (2 tsp) citric acid	Burgundy wine yeast and nutrient

Make in the same way as already described for canned apricots, etc. Store this wine for at least one year for it improves with keeping.

Bilberry and Blackberry Wine

500 g (1 lb) fresh bilberries	Pectic enzyme and Campden tablets
1 kg (2 lb) garden blackberries	3.5 litres (6 pints) water
2 ripe bananas	Burgundy wine yeast and nutrient
250 g (½ lb) raisins	
10 g (2 tsp) citric acid	
4 g (1 tsp) grape tannin	

Remove stalks, wash and crush the bilberries, blackberries and peeled bananas. Wash and chop the raisins.

Place the fruit in a bin, pour on hot water, cover and leave to cool.

Add the acid, pectic enzyme and one crushed Campden tablet, cover and leave for 24 hours.

Add the activated yeast, nutrient and tannin and ferment on the pulp for 4 days, keeping the fruit submerged.

Strain out, press and discard the pulp, stir in the sugar, pour the must into a jar, fit an airlock and continue the fermentation to dryness.

Rack, add one Campden tablet and store until the wine is bright. Rack again and store in bulk for at least one year before bottling, then keep for a further 6 months or longer.

Serve this wine free from chill with all red meat dishes.

NOTE Fewer bilberries may be used if no more are available. Make up with elderberries, stoned damsons, blackcurrants or sloes. Instead of pulp fermentation, the fruit and water may be heated to 80°C (175°F) for 15 minutes; cooled, strained and pressed; pulp discarded and fermented as juice.

Blackberry Wine

Blackberries are a favourite fruit for making red table wine. They blend very well with apples, blackcurrants, damsons, elderberries and sloes. Bananas or dried apricots add to the body and flavour of these blends. Garden blackberries are considered to be best for table wines. Hedgerow blackberries have a slightly strong flavour and are preferred for dessert wines.

2 kg (4 lb) garden blackberries	4 g (1 tsp) grape tannin
2 ripe bananas	Pectic enzyme and Campden tablets
250 g ($\frac{1}{2}$ lb) raisins	
1 kg (2 lb) white sugar	3.5 litres (6 pints) water
5 g (1 tsp) citric acid	Bordeaux wine yeast and nutrient

Remove stalks, wash and crush the blackberries, peel and mash the bananas, wash and chop the raisins. Place the fruit in a bin, pour on hot water, cover and leave to cool.

Add the acid, pectic enzyme and one crushed Campden tablet, cover and leave for 24 hours.

Add the activated yeast, nutrient and tannin and ferment on the pulp with the fruit submerged for 4 days.

Strain out and press the fruit, discard the pulp and stir in the sugar, pour the must into a jar, fit an airlock and continue fermentation to dryness.

Rack, add one Campden tablet, store until bright, then rack again. Mature this wine for one year in bulk and at least 6 months in bottle.

Autumn Harvest

1 kg (2 lb) garden blackberries	1 kg (2 lb) white sugar
250 g ($\frac{1}{2}$ lb) blackcurrants	5 g (1 tsp) citric acid
250 g ($\frac{1}{2}$ lb) choice elderberries	4 g (1 tsp) grape tannin
250 g ($\frac{1}{2}$ lb) stoned damsons or black plums	3.5 litres (6 pints) water
1 kg (2 lb) mixed apples	Burgundy wine yeast and nutrient
250 g ($\frac{1}{2}$ lb) raisins	

Remove stalks, wash, stone, crush or chop the fruit and place it in a bin of hot water. Cover and leave to cool.

Add the acid, pectic enzyme, and one crushed Campden tablet, cover and leave for 24 hours.

Add an activated yeast, nutrient and tannin and ferment on the pulp for 4 days with the fruit submerged.

Strain out and press and discard the pulp, stir in the sugar, pour the must into a fermentation jar, fit an airlock and continue fermentation to dryness.

Rack into a sterilised jar, add one Campden tablet and store until the wine is bright, then rack again.

Store this wine for a further year, at least, in bulk and another year in bottle.

This is a consistently good wine year after year, but it does need 2 years in which to mature. Make as much of this wine as possible, using whatever fruits are available to you. Fresh grapes could be included or a few bilberries, some ripe sloes and so on. The blackberries and blackcurrants can be cleaned and frozen as collected and kept until required. Thaw them only just before use. Fruits not available may be replaced by those that are.

Elderberry Wine

Sometimes described as the Englishman's grape, elderberries have long been used for making wine. There are at least 8 different varieties of elderberry but few people can tell one from another and nothing is known about the most suitable varieties for making wine. When gathering elderberries it is best to pick fruit from a number of different trees or bushes rather than from one alone. Gather only the black-ripe bunches and remove them from their stalks as quickly as possible. The juice of the berries stains everything with which it comes into contact, so you may wish to wear fine rubber gloves and an apron while handling this fruit.

The berries can be removed from the stalks with your fingers or with a stainless steel fork (see page 26). Comb them into a wide mouthed bowl or bin so that none fall onto the floor. Too many berries to the 5 litres (1 gallon) will make a very strongly flavoured wine that takes years to mature. It is customary to use fewer elderberries than other fruits in similar wines and to make up the body with bananas, blackberries and even dried apricots.

The best colour extraction is obtained by crushing the cleaned and washed berries and heating them in water. Boiling them whole until they 'dimple' – the method of our forebears – is better replaced by maintaining them at a temperature of 80°C (175°F) for 15 minutes. When cool, they can be strained and pressed and the pulp discarded. Fermentation on the pulp for too long extracts not only the colour but also a great deal of bitterness and is not recommended.

In addition to freshly gathered elderberries from hedgerows, dried elderberries can be bought from Home Brew shops. Although quite expensive, they have a four fold expansion and 500 g (1 lb) of dried elderberries is the equivalent of 2 kg (4 lb) of fresh elderberries – already gathered and stalked for you! Always wash them in a sulphite solution before use to remove dirt, dust and bacteria. They are best used in small quantities as an additive to other wines to which they contribute both colour and flavour. They benefit from the heat treatment already described.

Elderberry purée in cans is also available. It is extremely easy to use both by itself and as an additive to other wines. It is also available blended with rosehip purée to make an attractive wine. Detailed instructions are given with each pack.

1 kg (2 lb) ripe elderberries	2 g ($\frac{1}{2}$ tsp) grape tannin
250 g ($\frac{1}{2}$ lb) dried apricots	Pectic enzyme and Campden tablets
2 ripe bananas	4 litres ($6\frac{1}{2}$ pints) water
250 g ($\frac{1}{2}$ lb) raisins	
250 g (2 lb) white sugar	Bordeaux wine yeast and nutrient
15 g (3 tsp) citric acid	

Clean, wash and crush the elderberries, wash and chop the dried apricots and raisins and peel and slice the bananas. Place all the fruit in a preserving pan with the water. Heat and maintain a temperature of 80°C (175°F) for 15 minutes or so. Leave to cool.

Strain and press the fruit dry, discard the pulp and pour the liquor into a bin, stir in the acid, pectic enzyme and one crushed Campden tablet. Cover and leave for 24 hours.

Stir in the sugar, activated yeast, nutrient and tannin, pour the must into a fermentation jar, fit an airlock and ferment the wine to dryness.

Rack the clearing wine into a sterilised jar, add one Campden tablet, bung tight, label and store until bright. Rack again and store for at least one year before bottling, then keep it for a further year. If the wine finally tastes too dry for your palate, add one crushed saccharin tablet per bottle just prior to serving.

Elderberry and Apple Rosé

Quite often, apple wine is made at the same time as elderberry wine. Instead of discarding the two pulps, amalgamate them, add 5 litres (1 gallon) of cold water and a quarter can 250 g ($\frac{1}{2}$ lb) of concentrated white grape juice. One teaspoonful more of citric acid is needed.

The pulp will soon start to ferment from the yeast in the apple pulp. Keep the pulp submerged and well stirred for 5 days. Strain out, press dry and now discard the pulp, stir in 750 g (1½ lb) white sugar, pour the must into a jar, fit an airlock and ferment to dryness.

Rack, add one Campden tablet, bung, label and store until the wine is bright, then rack again and store for 6 months. Bottle and keep this wine for a month or two longer. Just prior to serving, add one crushed saccharin tablet per bottle to take the edge off the dryness, then serve this wine nicely chilled with buffet food. This is a remarkably successful rosé that can also be sparkled.

Folly

One of the more unusual wines, but a very successful one, is made from the leaves and shoots of blackberry bushes and grape vines. Much of the fruit flavour is also in the leaves and can be extracted. The name 'folly' is derived from the French word 'feuille' meaning leaf.

When pruning excess foliage from these plants in the summer, then, do not discard the young shoots and leaves, but turn them into wine. If it is not immediately convenient to do so, or if you have too few, they can be washed, sulphited, chopped up, packed into polythene bags and frozen for future use. Blackcurrant leaves also have a very strong flavour and can be blended in. Old or coarse leaves are not suitable. Use only young, tender and fresh looking leaves and shoots that have not recently been sprayed with a fungicide.

3 kg (6 lb) vine and/ or bramble shoots and leaves	14 g (2½ tsp) citric acid
250 g (½ lb) concentrated white grape juice	2 g (½ tsp) grape tannin
2 ripe bananas	4 litres (6½ pints) water
825 g (1¾ lb) white sugar	Hock wine yeast and nutrient

Wash the leaves and shoots, chop them up small and place them in a preserving pan of boiling water. Add the peeled and thinly sliced bananas and simmer gently for half an hour. Turn over or stir up the leaves from time to time. Leave to cool.

Strain out and press and discard the leaves and stir in the grape juice, sugar, activated yeast, nutrient and tannin. Pour the must into a fermentation jar, top up, fit an airlock and ferment to dryness.

Rack, add one Campden tablet and store until the wine is bright. Rack again and store in bulk for 6 months before bottling. Keep the wine for a few months longer, then serve chilled like any other white table wine. When slightly sweetened just before serving, this is an attractive wine to drink on its own.

1 kg (2 lb) canned gooseberries in syrup	2 g ($\frac{1}{2}$ tsp) grape tannin
250 g ($\frac{1}{2}$ lb) sultanas	Pectic enzyme and Campden tablets
1 ripe banana	3.5 litres (6 pints) water
750 g ($1\frac{1}{2}$ lb) white sugar	Hock yeast and nutrient
10 g (2 tsp) citric acid	

Gooseberry Wine

There is no doubt among experienced wine-makers that gooseberries make many of the best white table wines, comparing very highly with commercial wines. The small to medium sized 'Careless' variety makes a fine dry wine reminiscent of a Moselle wine. The larger 'Leveller' makes a fuller bodied wine reminiscent of the white wines from Bordeaux. Dessert gooseberries can also be used, although their strong flavour tends to remain pronounced in the wine. If left on their bushes to become over-ripe, they can be made into a splendid sweet wine that needs long keeping to earn the best reward.

Canned gooseberries quickly produce a very attractive light wine by themselves and blend effectively with other fruits as well. Catering packs can frequently be obtained for making larger quantities of wine. It is worthwhile making canned gooseberry wine first because it matures quickly. This not only encourages you to make wine from fresh gooseberries but also provides you with some wine to drink in the meantime.

Although the following recipes are given for 5 litres (1 gallon) you are recommended to make larger quantities if you can. The fresh fruit version can take anything from one to 3 years to mature and the great danger is that they will be drunk too soon. Store some of these wines in half size bottles so that you can monitor their progress before they reach their peak.

Strain the gooseberry syrup into a sterilised bottle and keep it in the refrigerator until it is required.

Mash the gooseberries and put them in a bin together with the washed and chopped sultanas and the peeled and thinly sliced banana, the acid, pectic enzyme, one crushed Campden tablet and the water. Cover and leave for 24 hours.

Add the syrup, activated yeast, nutrient and tannin, and ferment on the pulp for 3 days keeping the fruit submerged.

Strain out, press and discard the fruit, stir in the sugar, pour the must into a fermentation jar, fit an airlock and continue the fermentation to the end.

Rack into a sterilised jar, add one Campden tablet and store until the wine is bright.

Siphon into sterilised bottles and keep them in a cool place until the wine is 3–4 months old before serving it nicely chilled.

Gooseberry Wine (2)

1.75 kg ($3\frac{1}{2}$ lb) 'Careless' gooseberries	2 g ($\frac{1}{2}$ tsp) grape tannin
250 g ($\frac{1}{2}$ lb) sultanas	Pectic enzyme and Campden tablets
1 kg (2 lb) white sugar	4 litres (7 pints) water
5 g (1 tsp) citric acid	Burgundy wine yeast and nutrient

Select gooseberries that are ripe but still green and firm.

Top, tail and wash the gooseberries, put them in a bin, pour hot water over them, cover and leave to cool.

Crush the gooseberries with your hands or a potato masher.

Wash and chop the sultanas and add to the bin, together with the acid, pectic enzyme and one crushed Campden tablet. Cover and leave for 24 hours.

Add an activated yeast, nutrient and tannin and ferment on the pulp for three days keeping the fruit submerged.

Strain out, press and discard the fruit, stir in the sugar, pour the must into a jar, fit an airlock and continue the fermentation.

Rack, add one Campden tablet and store until bright, then rack again. Store for one year in bulk and 6 months in bottle. Serve cold with fish, poultry or pork.

Gooseberry Wine (3)

1.75 kg (3½ lb) 'Leveller' gooseberries	2 g (½ tsp) grape tannin
250 g (½ lb) sultanas	Pectic enzyme and Campden tablets
2 ripe bananas	4 litres (6½ pints) water
1.5 kg (2½ lb) white sugar	Sauternes wine yeast and nutrient
10 g (2 tsp) citric acid	

Select fully ripe and slightly soft gooseberries.

Top, tail, wash and crush them, peel and mash the bananas, wash and chop the sultanas. Put all the fruit in a bin of cold water containing the acid, pectic enzyme and one crushed Campden tablet. Cover and leave for 24 hours.

Stir well, remove a jugful of pulp and juice, strain it into a trial jar and check the specific gravity with a hydrometer. Make a note of the reading on the record card.

Return the pulp and juice to the bin and mix in the activated yeast, nutrient and tannin. Ferment on the pulp for 3 days keeping the pulp submerged.

Strain out and press the pulp and discard, check the gravity of the must and stir in sufficient sugar to achieve a total specific gravity of 1.110. See page 31 for further details.

Pour the must into a fermentation jar, fit an airlock and continue the fermentation until the specific gravity has fallen to 1.020, after about 2 weeks, but check every few days.

Rack the wine into a sterilised jar containing one gram of potassium sorbate and one crushed Campden tablet, stir in some proprietary finings and leave the wine in a cool place to clear.

When the wine is bright, rack again and store for at least one year in bulk and a further 6–9 months in bottle. Serve it cold with the dessert course of a meal.

Grape Wine

Many people now grow a few grape vines in their gardens and in the summer imported grapes can often be bought at reasonable prices. It is best to assemble a mixture of different grapes and some 8 to 9 kg (16 to 18 lb) are needed to make 5 litres (1 gallon) of wine. Remove stalks, wash and crush the grapes, add one crushed Campden tablet and pectic enzyme. Cover and leave for 24 hours.

Next day, the white grapes can be strained through a nylon bag and pressed dry and the pulp discarded.

Black grapes can be heated to 80°C (175°F) for fifteen minutes, then cooled, strained, pressed and the pulp discarded.

If any of the grapes, white or black, are over-ripe or mouldy, it is best to submit them to the heat treatment.

When the juice has been assembled, check the specific gravity and, if needs be, stir in sufficient sugar to achieve a reading between 1.080 and 1.090. Home grown grapes are unlikely to need any acid, but bought in grapes may be very ripe and therefore in need of 5 g (1 teaspoonful) of citric acid per 5 litres (1 gallon).

Mix in an active wine yeast of your choice and ferment the wine to dryness under an airlock.

Rack, add one Campden tablet per 5 litres (1 gallon), fine and when the wine is bright, rack again. Store in bulk for at least 6 months and in bottle for a further 3–6 months.

Mixed Soft Fruits Wine

In the early summer, a wealth of soft fruits becomes available to the winemaker. They include raspberries, strawberries, gooseberries, black, red and white currants, loganberries, garden blackberries, cherries and so on. The demands from the family to eat the fruit fresh is so difficult to resist that often there is only a small quantity of each fruit available for winemaking. Happily, a mixture of all these small quantities makes a delicious rosé wine that should not be missed. The important fact is to use as many different fruits as you can and not too much of any single fruit.

1.75 kg (3½ lb) mixed soft fruits	2.5 litres (4 pints) water
250 g (½ lb) concentrated grape juice	Bordeaux wine yeast and nutrient
825 g (1¾ lb) white sugar	Acid and tannin as necessary
Pectic enzyme and Campden tablets	

Remove stalks, wash, stone and crush the fruit and put it in a bin containing the water, pectic enzyme and one crushed Campden tablet. Cover and leave for 24 hours.

Stir in the concentrated grape juice of your choice – red, white or rosé, depending on the colour of the fruit. If the assembly contains blackberries and or blackcurrants, use white or rosé concentrate.

Add an activated yeast and nutrient and ferment on the pulp for 3 days keeping the pulp submerged.

Strain out, press and discard the fruit, stir in the sugar, pour the must into a fermentation jar, fit an airlock and ferment down to specific gravity 1.002. Alternatively, ferment the wine to dryness and sweeten it with one or 2 saccharine tablets per bottle just prior to serving it chilled.

Rack into a sterilised jar containing one gram (¼ tsp) of potassium sorbate and one crushed Campden tablet to terminate fermentation. Add some wine finings (see page 35) and as soon as the wine is bright, rack again.

Store this wine for one year before bottling, then keep for a few months longer.

Orange Wine

All the different varieties of oranges, clementines, mandarins, satsumas, tangerines and ortaniques can be made into wine. The one important point to remember is that all the white pith must be excluded. The wine is made from the juice and the very thinly pared rinds. Firm skinned oranges can be pared with a sharp potato knife. Loose skinned oranges are best peeled and cleaned from the inside by scraping away and discarding the pith until only the orange coloured skin remains. If white pith does get into the must, it imparts a distinct and unpleasant bitterness to the wine. It is also very rich in pectin and will cause the wine to be hazy. Once again it seems best to use a selection of different varieties. The bitter Seville orange for example is best used in equal proportions with sweet oranges like the 'Navel', rather than on its own.

10 sweet oranges	3.5 litres (6 pints) water
250 g (¼ can) concentrated white grape juice	Sauternes wine yeast and nutrient
750 g (1½ lb) white sugar	

Wipe over the oranges with a sulphited cloth, thinly pare them and chop the parings into small pieces. Halve the oranges and express the juice; strain this through a nylon sieve.

Mix the parings, orange juice, grape juice, sugar, water and activated yeast and nutrient together and when the sugar is quite dissolved, pour the must into a fermentation jar, fit an airlock and ferment out.

Rack into a sterilised jar, add one Campden tablet and store the wine until it is bright. Rack again and keep for one year before bottling. Serve this wine nicely chilled with duck, chicken or pork dishes.

Plum Wine

All the different varieties of plums can be used for making wine, including dried plums – prunes. Ripe fruit is the best to use because the stones can be extracted more easily. After removing the stalks, the plums should be washed in hot water containing a little household soda to remove the waxy bloom. A rinse in running cold water removes any lingering trace of soda. If not removed, the bloom is often carried forward into the finished wine. Unless removed, the stones impart a distinctive and unpleasant taste to the wine.

Greengages and golden or egg plums make a fine dry white wine, damsons and black plums make good red wines both for table and dessert purposes. Victoria plums and prunes make excellent aperitif wines in the sherry style and are included on page 55.

2 kg (4 lb) stoned greengages and/or golden or egg plums	Pectic enzyme and Campden tablets
250 g (½ lb) sultanas	3.5 litres (6 pints) water
2 ripe bananas	Burgundy wine yeast and nutrient
1 kg (2 lb) white sugar	
5 g (1 tsp) citric acid	
2 g (½ tsp) grape tannin	

Prepare the fruit as indicated above, peel and mash the bananas, wash and chop the sultanas, put them in a bin containing the water, acid, pectic enzyme and one crushed Campden tablet. Cover and leave for 24 hours.

Add the activated yeast, nutrient and tannin and ferment on the pulp for 3 days, keeping the fruit submerged.

Strain out and press and discard the pulp, stir in the sugar, pour the must into a fermentation jar, fit an airlock and ferment out to dryness.

Rack the clearing wine into a sterilised jar, add one Campden tablet and when the wine is bright, rack again.

Store this wine for 9 months in bulk and 6 months in bottle. Serve cold with fish, poultry or pork.

Strawberry Jam Wine

Although fresh strawberries usually make a poor wine, strawberry jam consistently makes a good rosé. Use pure jam containing only fruit, sugar and water. Avoid jams that contain added pectin, colouring and preservatives. Because of the pectin in the jam you must use double the usual quantity of pectic enzyme.

1.5 kg (3 lb) strawberry jam	2 g (½ tsp) grape tannin
250 g (½ lb) concentrated rosé grape juice	Pectic enzyme and Campden tablets
500 g (1 lb) white sugar	4 litres (6 pints) water
10 g (2 tsp) citric acid	Bordeaux wine yeast and nutrient

Dissolve the jam in the warm water and when cool mix in the acid, double quantity of pectic enzyme and one crushed Campden tablet. Cover and leave for 24 hours.

Stir in the grape juice, activated yeast, nutrient and tannin and ferment for 2 days. Strain out the pulp, discard, stir in the sugar and pour the must into a fermentation jar. Fit an airlock and ferment out.

When fermentation is finished and the wine begins to clear, rack into a sterilised jar, add one Campden tablet and store until the wine is bright. Rack again and store the wine in bulk for 3 months, then bottle and keep it for a month or two longer.

Slightly sweeten this wine with one or two saccharin tablets per bottle just prior to serving it nicely chilled with buffet food.

Peach Wine

A splendid sweet table wine can be made from peaches. Often a whole tray can be bought from the greengrocer, some of which may be over-ripe and very juicy.

2.5 kg (5 lb) fresh peaches	2 g ($\frac{1}{2}$ tsp) grape tannin
2 ripe bananas	Pectic enzyme and Campden tablets
250 g ($\frac{1}{2}$ lb) concentrated white grape juice	4 litres (7 pints) water
1 kg (2 lb) white sugar	Sauternes wine yeast and nutrient
10 g (2 tsp) citric acid	

Cut the peaches in halves over a sterilised bin, remove and discard the stones, peel off and discard the skins, chop up, crush or liquidise the fruit and add to the water.

Peel, crush or liquidise the bananas, add the grape juice (Sauternes style for preference), the citric acid, pectic enzyme and one crushed Campden tablet. Cover and leave for 24 hours.

Add an activated yeast, nutrient and tannin, loosely cover the bin and ferment on the pulp for 3 days, keeping the pulp submerged.

Strain out the pulp in a nylon bag or sieve, roll it round and round, but do not press it. Discard. Stir in the sugar, pour the must into a fermentation jar, fit an airlock and ferment down to specific gravity of 1.010.

Rack the wine into a clean jar containing 1 gram ($\frac{1}{4}$ tsp) of potassium sorbate and one crushed Campden tablet to terminate fermentation. Add some wine finings, leave the wine in a cool place and as soon as it is bright, rack again.

Store the wine in bulk for 6 months, then bottle it and keep it for a further 6 months. Serve it nicely chilled with the dessert course.

Instead of terminating fermentation at specific gravity of 1.010, the wine may be fermented out, racked and sweetened to taste with 175 g (6 oz) lactose, an unfermentable sugar that is only one-third as sweet as household sugar. Alternatively, saccharin may be used just prior to serving.

Peach Pulp Wine

Sometimes, catering-size cans of peach pulp or pieces can be bought from cash and carry outlets which make a good wine. They should be used at the rate of 1.5 kg (3 lb) to 5 litres (1 gallon) of wine. Don't forget the bananas and grape concentrate since these help to produce a full-bodied wine.

Raisin Wine

As far back as 1635, Thomas Chamberlayne obtained permission to make and sell wines from 'raysons'. They have continued to make good wine ever since. About two-thirds of their weight consists of fermentable sugar. One measure of raisins is the equivalent of 4 measures of grapes. Raisins vary in quality from year to year and also from one centre of production to another. As a result the wine can also vary slightly – from good to splendid!

2 kg (4 lb) raisins	5 litres (1 gallon) water, approx.
5 g (1 tsp) citric acid	
2 g ($\frac{1}{2}$ tsp) grape tannin	Madeira wine yeast

Wash the raisins in a sulphite solution, chop them up, place them in a bin with the citric acid and grape tannin. Pour on 4 litres (7 pints) of warm but not hot water. When cool add an activated yeast.

Ferment on the pulp for 10 days, keeping the pulp well submerged the whole time.

Strain out and press the fruit as dry as you can, discard and pour the must into a fermentation jar, top up with cold boiled water, fit an airlock and ferment out.

Rack the wine into a clean jar, add one Campden tablet, bung tight, label and store until the wine is bright. Rack again and store for a total of 6 months in bulk. Then bottle and store for a further 3 months or so.

Before serving this wine, sweeten it to taste with demerara sugar. It has a tawny-gold hue and is reminiscent of the wines from Madeira.

Sultana Wine

Sultanas make a lighter wine that is very attractive when chilled and served with gammon or baked ham. Use the same quantity of sultanas as recommended for raisins and make the wine in the same way as indicated for raisin wine.

Redcurrant Wine

Although not as popular as blackcurrants, redcurrants are widely grown by gardeners and can often be bought from the greengrocer. The fruit makes a very fresh-tasting rosé wine.

1.5 kg (3 lb) redcurrants	Pectic enzyme and Campden tablets
250 g (½ lb) sultanas	4 litres (7 pints) water
2 ripe bananas	
1 kg (2 lb) white sugar	Bordeaux wine yeast and nutrient
2 g (½ tsp) grape tannin	(No acid is required)

Remove stalks, wash and crush the currants, wash and chop the sultanas, peel and mash the bananas and place them all in a bin containing the water, pectic enzyme and one crushed Campden tablet. Cover the bin and leave it in a warm place for 24 hours.

Stir in an activated yeast, nutrient and tannin and ferment on the pulp for 4 days keeping the pulp submerged and the bin loosely covered.

Strain out, press dry and discard the fruit, stir in the sugar, pour the must into a fermentation jar, fit an airlock and ferment down to specific gravity of 1.004.

Rack the wine into a clean fermentation jar containing one crushed Campden tablet and 1 gram (¼ tsp) of potassium sorbate to terminate fermentation. Stir in some finings, leave the jar in a cool place and as soon as the wine is bright, rack again.

Store this wine in bulk for 6 months, then bottle it and keep it for a further 6 months. Serve it cold with buffet food.

NOTE Instead of terminating fermentation as described, the wine may be fermented to dryness and slightly sweetened with one or, at the most, 2 saccharin tablets per bottle just before serving.

A redcurrant syrup can sometimes be bought in chemists and health food shops. One 340 ml (12 fl oz) bottle is sufficient for 5 litres (1 gallon) of wine. Canned or bottled redcurrants may also be used.

Rhubarb Wine

2 kg (4 lb) rhubarb stalks	2 g (½ tsp) grape tannin
250 g (½ lb) dried apricots	Pectic enzyme and Campden tablets
250 g (½ lb) sultanas	4 litres (7 pints) water
1 kg (2 lb) white sugar	Burgundy wine yeast and nutrient
1 large fresh lemon	

Cut off the leaf and the top of the stem as well as the white foot of each stalk. Wipe them clean with a cloth dipped in a sulphite solution and chop them into thin rings. The finished weight should be as recommended above. Place the rhubarb in a bin together with the washed and chopped apricots and sultanas. Very thinly pare the lemon and add the parings to the bin. Pour on hot water, cover and leave to cool. Add the pectic enzyme, the expressed lemon juice and one crushed Campden tablet, cover and leave for 24 hours.

Stir in the activated yeast, nutrient and tannin and ferment on the pulp for 4 days, keeping the fruit submerged.

Strain out and press the fruit dry, discard the pulp and stir in the sugar, pour the must into a fermentation jar, fit an airlock and ferment out.

Rack into a clean jar, add one Campden tablet, bung tight, label and store until the wine is bright. Rack again, store in bulk for 6 months, then bottle and keep for a further few months.

Serve this fresh, clean, dry white wine nicely chilled, with fish, poultry and pork dishes. The individual fruit flavours blend well and are indiscernible.

Aperitifs

The English meaning of the French word 'aperitif' is appetiser, a word that lacks the aesthetic appeal of the French. Nevertheless, the English word clearly indicates that this before-a-meal drink is intended to stimulate one's appetite for the meal to come. It follows, then, that the drink should be mouth cleansing, fresh tasting, slightly bitter and dry – or nearly so. The most popular aperitifs are vermouth, sherry, dry white wine, gin and tonic, sparkling wine and beer – depending on the occasion and the company. Sparkling wine and beer are covered in other chapters. So, too, in a sense, is dry white wine, for many white table wines are suitable for serving as an aperitif as well as with the meal. But there are certain fruits, notably grapefruit and pineapple which make wines that are particularly suitable for serving as aperitifs.

Vermouth

Vermouths are not widely made at home for some reason, although there are some excellent, appropriately flavoured, concentrated grape juices on the market and they are made up in the same way as any other kit wine. Each manufacturer gives precise directions on the label for making the wine. Several different styles are available including dry white, sweet white, sweet red, French and Italian.

Occasionally one can find sachets of herbs suitably blended to add to an appropriate wine during a prolonged fermentation to make a strong wine. The herbs include, camomile,

Kits for three different styles of vermouth and a ginora

clove, coriander, hyssop, juniper, orange peel, quinine and wormwood. The wine takes its name from 'vermut' – the German word for wormwood. The precise quantities of each herb used by commercial manufacturers vary and give each brand its own individual character.

Ginora

Another attractive, juniper flavoured, grape concentrate is Ginora. It is made up in the same way as other kits and detailed instructions are given on the label. When fermentation is finished and the wine has cleared, from a quarter to a full bottle of gin may be added to increase the alcohol content and emphasise the flavour a little more. The finished wine is as strong as a gin and tonic and needs only a slice of lemon to give it its final piquancy. The flavour is remarkably accurate and for gin and tonic lovers, Ginora produces a highly successful substitute showing a very substantial saving of tax.

Sherry-style

Sherry type wines are much more popular with amateur winemakers and some surprisingly realistic results can be achieved. Genuine sherry from Spain is a blend of wines from different years. One year a sherry producer lays down a line of giant-sized casks of wine. The following year he lays down another and the third year another and so on. He then sells one third of the wine from each cask of the first year and replaces that wine from his second year casks which he replenishes from his third year casks and so on. Each year another third is sold from the first year casks and replaced as just described. The older wine is refreshed by the younger wine and imparts its own distinctive character to it in return. Very soon the wine coming from the first casks tastes the same every year. There are no variations due to the season. Every year is consequently a good year.

During fermentation the wine achieves a natural alcohol content of around 14% and is fortified to 17 or 18% with grape spirit. The casks are never completely filled so that the air space causes the wine to oxidise. Frequently a special yeast will grow on the surface of the wine and this, too, imparts a distinctive flavour to the dry or 'fino' sherries. Some are sweetened slightly to make a medium dry/sweet sherry called 'amontillado', others are sweetened still more to make cream or 'oloroso' sherries.

In the home this process can be copied, with care and patience, but few amateur winemakers follow completely the blending methods described. Many make a single sherry-like wine with great success, choosing suitable fruits and vegetables, fermenting them with a sherry yeast so they become as strong as possible and then maturing them in containers not quite full. A number of suitable recipes can be made up in the course of a season or two and blended together in a single large container to produce an even more sherry-like wine.

Adequate storage is essential, however, to obtain the best results, especially if the wine has been fermented on and even fortified to achieve an alcohol content of 17 or 18%. Full details of how to do this are given in the chapter on dessert wines.

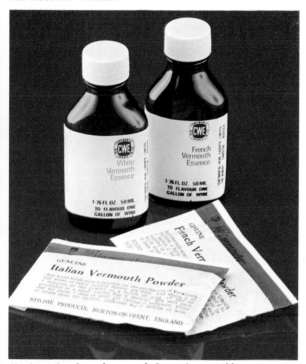

Bottles and sachets of vermouth flavourings to add to any strong, bland wine

Ingredients

The most successful recipes include a number of different ingredients and many include some gypsum and cream of tartar to improve the acidity and flavour. A good sherry yeast is essential. The wine should be fermented with sufficient acid, nutrient, sugar and warmth to produce a high alcohol content. It should then be cleared and matured for a minimum of one year in a container not quite full and plugged with cotton wool rather than a bung. This enables air to filter in and provides the wine with oxygen, so that it can develop the distinctive sherry flavour.

Winemaids

When vermouth, ginora and sherry-like aperitifs are made and ready for drinking, they can be suitably stored in *Winemaid* cartons rather than bottles. For everyday use you often need only two or three glasses of aperitif at a time. Indeed, you may need just one glass of each aperitif to suit the different tastes of the family. By storing these wines in a Winemaid carton, you can remove as little as one glassful at a time over a period of months, confident in the knowledge that the rest of the wine will not deteriorate. Three such cartons each with a different aperitif and kept in the refrigerator, can provide you with a glass of 'vermouth', 'gin and tonic' or 'sherry' at the press of a button. For the family fond of an aperitif before their meal, this method combines the latest technology with enormous economy. It can be recommended unreservedly.

Pineapple and Grapefruit

1 large can unsweetened grapefruit juice (approx. 1.35 litres/40 fl oz)	250 g ($\frac{1}{4}$ can) concentrated white grape juice
1 large can unsweetened pineapple juice (approx. 1.35 litres/40 fl oz)	1 kg (2 lb) white or Demerara sugar
	1.5 litres ($2\frac{1}{2}$ pints) water
	Madeira wine yeast and nutrient

Mix all the ingredients together, pour the must into a fermentation jar, fit an airlock and ferment out to dryness.

Rack into a sterilised jar, add one Campden tablet, bung tight, label and store until the wine is bright.

Rack again and store the wine in a cool place until it is 6 months old. Bottle it and store for a few weeks longer or store it in a Winemaid carton. Serve it cold with savoury biscuits.

Bitter Orange

4 Seville oranges (bitter)	3.5 litres (6 pints) water
4 Navel oranges (sweet)	Pectic enzyme and Campden tablets
4 cooking apples	Sherry yeast and nutrient
4 ripe bananas	
250 g ($\frac{1}{2}$ lb) sultanas	
1.375 kg ($2\frac{3}{4}$ lb) white sugar	

Wash the apples, oranges and sultanas in a sulphite solution.

Thinly pare the oranges, halve the husks, express and strain the juice. Chop the peel and place it in a bin together with the juice, the water, the pectic enzyme and one crushed Campden tablet.

Chop the sultanas, peel and mash the bananas, crush the apples and add all these to the bin. Cover and leave it for 24 hours.

Add an activated sherry yeast and nutrient and ferment on the pulp for 4 days keeping the fruit cap submerged and the bin covered.

Strain out and press the fruit dry, discard the pulp, stir in half the sugar, pour the must into a fermentation jar, plug the neck with cotton wool instead of an airlock and ferment down to specific gravity of 1.002.

Stir in half the remaining sugar and again ferment down to specific gravity of 1.002.

Repeat this process and provided the fermentation is still active, stir in the rest of the sugar. Check the specific gravity regularly. The aim is to keep the fermentation going as long as possible, if necessary with a little more sugar, but to finish the wine with a reading of 1.000.

When the wine begins to clear, rack it into a clean jar, leaving some airspace above the wine. Do *not* add a Campden tablet nor use a bung. Instead, plug the neck of the jar with cotton wool. Any excess wine should be stored in a suitably sized bottle also plugged with cotton wool. Both jar and bottle should be filled only to the shoulder.

When the wine is bright, rack it again into similar containers and store it for at least one year and preferably two. It may then be bottled or kept in a Winemaid carton.

Serve this sherry-like wine slightly chilled with canapés.

Grape and Banana

8 kg (16 lb) Cypriot seedless grapes
250 g ($\frac{1}{2}$ lb) bananas
2 lemons
750 g (1$\frac{1}{2}$ lb) white sugar
30 g (1 oz) gypsum
15 g ($\frac{1}{2}$ oz) cream of tartar
2 g ($\frac{1}{2}$ tsp) grape tannin
Pectic enzyme and Campden tablets
Sherry yeast and nutrient

Remove the main stalk, wash and crush the grapes and place them in a polythene bin. Peel and mash the ripe bananas and add to the bin. Thinly pare, chop and add the lemon rind, halve the husks, express and add the juice. Add the pectic enzyme and one crushed Campden tablet, cover and leave for 24 hours.

Add an activated sherry yeast and nutrient, the gypsum and cream of tartar and ferment on the pulp for 3 days, keeping the fruit cap submerged and the bin covered.

Strain out and press the fruit dry, discard the pulp and stir in one third of the sugar. Pour the must into a fermentation jar, leave an airspace and plug the neck with cotton wool.

Continue the prolonged fermentation as described for Bitter Orange Wine and finish the wine dry. Serve it cold with nuts or canapés.

Parsnip, Fig and Raisin

2 kg (4 lb) parsnips
500 g (1 lb) raisins
250 g ($\frac{1}{2}$ lb) dried figs
1.25 kg (2$\frac{1}{2}$ lb) white sugar
2 lemons
10 g (2 tsp) citric acid
4 g (1 tsp) grape tannin
30 g (1 oz) gypsum
15 g ($\frac{1}{2}$ oz) cream of tartar
4 litres (7 pints) water
Pectic enzyme and Campden tablets
Sherry yeast and nutrient

Scrub the parsnips, discard the crowns, dice and boil them with the thinly pared rinds of the lemons until they are tender. Leave to cool.

Strain out the vegetables and lemon rind, add the washed and chopped raisins and the washed and broken figs to the liquor. Stir in the citric acid, lemon juice, pectic enzyme and one crushed Campden tablet. Cover and leave for 24 hours.

Add the grape tannin, gypsum, cream of tartar, activated yeast and nutrient. Ferment on the pulp for 5 days keeping the fruit submerged and the bin loosely covered.

Strain out and press the fruit dry and discard the pulp, stir in half the sugar, pour the must into a fermentation jar and plug the neck with cotton wool.

Add the rest of the sugar during the fermentation as already described for Bitter Orange Wine. After 2 years this is a very good sherry-like wine. Serve it cold with savoury tit-bits.

Prune, Apricot and Raisin

1.5 kg (3 lb) best prunes
250 g ($\frac{1}{2}$ lb) dried apricots
250 g ($\frac{1}{2}$ lb) raisins
1.375 kg (2$\frac{3}{4}$ lb) white sugar
10 g (2 tsp) citric acid
2 g ($\frac{1}{4}$ tsp) grape tannin
30 g (1 oz) gypsum
15 g ($\frac{1}{2}$ oz) cream of tartar
Pectic enzyme and Campden tablets
Sherry yeast and nutrient

Wash the prunes, apricots and raisins, cut them up, place them in a bin and pour hot water over them. Cover and leave to cool.

Add the acid, pectic enzyme and one crushed Campden tablet, cover and leave for 24 hours.

Add the gypsum, cream of tartar, tannin, nutrient and activated sherry yeast. Ferment on the pulp for 4 days keeping the fruit cap submerged and the bin loosely covered.

Strain out and press the fruit dry and discard the pulp, stir in half the sugar, pour the must into a fermentation jar and plug the neck with cotton wool.

Continue as described for Bitter Orange.

A Winemaid with ingredients for a sherry-type wine

Rosehip and Fig

250 g (½ lb) dried rosehip shells
125 g (¼ lb) dried figs
250 g (½ lb) ripe bananas
250 g (½ lb) sultanas
2 lemons
1.375 kg (2¾ lb) white sugar
2 g (½ tsp) grape tannin

30g (1 oz) gypsum
15 g (½ oz) cream of tartar
Pectic enzyme and Campden tablets
4 litres (7 pints) water
Sherry yeast and nutrient

Wash the rosehip shells, figs and sultanas. Break up the figs, chop the sultanas, thinly pare the lemons and place them with the rosehip shells in a bin, together with the peeled and mashed bananas. Pour hot water over them, cover and leave them to cool.

Add the pectic enzyme, one crushed Campden tablet and the expressed juice of the 2 lemons. Cover and leave for 24 hours.

Add the gypsum, cream of tartar, grape tannin, nutrient and an activated sherry yeast. Ferment on the pulp for 4 days keeping the pulp submerged and the bin loosely covered. Strain out and press the pulp dry and discard, stir in half the sugar, pour the must into a fermentation jar and plug the neck with cotton wool.

Continue the fermentation as described for Bitter Orange.

This is a very popular recipe and if it is slightly sweetened after fermentation, produces an amontillado-like wine. Serve it cool.

Victoria Plum

3 kg (6 lb) ripe Victoria plums
250 g (½ lb) concentrated grape juice (dry sherry style)
1.375 kg (2¾ lb) white sugar
10 g (2 tsp) citric acid

2 g (½ tsp) grape tannin
Pectic enzyme and Campden tablets
3.5 litres (5½ pints) water
Sherry yeast and nutrient

Remove stalks, wash, stone and crush the plums. Place them in a bin with the acid, pectic enzyme, one crushed Campden tablet and the water. Cover and leave for 24 hours.

Stir in the concentrated grape juice, tannin, nutrient and an activated yeast. Ferment on the pulp for 4 days keeping the pulp submerged and the bin loosely covered.

Strain out and press the fruit dry and discard the pulp, stir in half the sugar, pour the must into a fermentation jar, plug the neck with cotton wool and continue the fermentation as described for Bitter Orange.

Sparkling wines

Although champagne has long been called the king of wines and the wine for kings, sparkling wine is not as widely made in the home as it deserves to be. It is no more difficult to make than any other wine; it can be cleared from its second sediment with ease and it tastes as fine as many commercial sparkling wines. Apples, gooseberries, pears, redcurrants and rhubarb all make excellent sparkling wines. Mead, too, can be sparkled very effectively. Indeed, almost any light table wine can be made into an attractive sparkling wine.

(left) Check the specific gravity – reading 0.992 meaning wine completely dry
(right) Add precisely 85 g per 5 litres (2½ oz per 1 gallon) sugar and an active champagne yeast

You can, of course, sparkle your wine simply by impregnating it with carbon dioxide in a soda siphon or even in a draught beer keg fitted with a carbon dioxide injector. It is much better however, to make it by the true champagne method.

Equipment

First of all you need to gather together some heavy champagne or sparkling wine bottles. No other wine bottle will do, since none is strong enough. The proper bottles can often be obtained from restaurants and hotels that cater for wedding parties. A case of a dozen bottles should not be difficult to acquire if you ask the right person in a kindly manner. Make

sure that every bottle is free from scratches and chips since these weaken the bottle. Equally important, soak off the labels without scratching the glass with the blade of a knife.

Next, you need to acquire some suitable stoppers and wire cages. Your Home Brew shop can provide hollow-domed plastic stoppers and the traditional wire cages to fasten the stoppers to the bottles. Some shops may stock the special stoppers with a blister attached in which the sediment from the secondary fermentation can be collected and then sealed off. The proper bottles with suitable stoppers and cages are the only specialised pieces of equipment that you need. It must be emphasised, however, that these are essential and that ordinary wine bottles and corks are quite unsuitable. The pressure from the secondary fermentation could burst an ordinary wine bottle, especially at the moment when the bottle is moved and the gas in the wine is disturbed. Lemonade, cider and beer bottles are made to withstand a lower pressure and, apart from not being strong enough, are aesthetically unacceptable. All other wines can be served from a decanter, but sparkling wines must by their nature be served from their bottles.

Ingredients

The best sparkling wines are intended as such from the outset. Proper consideration can then be given to the fruit content, to the yeast used and to the complete fermentation of the correct quantity of sugar. Since the wine has to undergo a second fermentation, the initial alcohol content ought not to exceed 11% at the maximum. To this end, an original specific gravity between 1.076 and 1.082 should be achieved.

Make the wine in the usual way, preferably using only just-ripe fruit rather than over-ripe fruit. A champagne yeast bestows the right base for the future flavour, but any wine yeast may be used at this stage. Make sure that the must contains sufficient acid and nutrient to effect a complete fermentation to dryness. When fermentation is finished, the specific gravity reading should be 0.994 or lower.

The second fermentation

After racking the wine, add one Campden tablet to prevent oxidation and infection, then mature it in a cool place for 6 months. By this time the wine should be crystal clear. If the jar contains any deposit, the clear wine should be siphoned into a sterilised jar. Now comes the process of secondary fermentation. A very precise amount of sugar must be added to the wine. Too little and the wine has insufficient sparkle and soon becomes flat and lifeless. Too much and the pressure can force out the wine as foam – or even burst the bottle. The safe and suitable quantity to add is 85 g per 5 litres (2½ oz per 1 gallon). In addition to providing the right amount of sparkle, this quantity of sugar also produces another 1% of alcohol.

Remove some wine, dissolve the sugar in it (caster sugar dissolves more readily than granulated sugar) and return the sweetened wine to the jar. Next, add the contents of a packet of champagne wine yeast and nutrient. For preference use a Haut Villier strain, but any champagne yeast will do. It is important to use a champagne yeast as opposed to any

other wine yeast, baker's yeast or brewer's yeast. The champagne wine yeast is better able to ferment under pressure and settles more cleanly and firmly than any other type of yeast. Furthermore, it bestows on the wine its own very special and characteristic flavour.

Dried yeast should first be activated in a little cold boiled water – a tablespoonful or two will be enough. Liquid yeast could be activated in a similar quantity of fruit juice or even added direct to the sweetened wine. An airlock must be fitted and the jar of wine stood in a warm place for a few hours until it can be seen that fermentation has started.

The sparkling wine bottles should then be sterilised, drained and filled to within 5cm (2in) of the top of the bottle. Some space must be left for expansion and pressure. Sterilised stoppers are then fitted and wired on to the bottles with cages. Label the bottles with details of the contents and dates. Lay them on their sides in a warm place for a few days until fermentation is complete, then store them still on their sides in a cool place for a minimum of 6 months and preferably one year.

Removing the sediment

A firm sediment will be seen on the side of each bottle and this has to be moved into the hollow dome of the stopper or into the blister attached to the stopper. To this end, place the bottles upside down in a bottle carton fixed in a position halfway between the vertical and the horizontal. Give each bottle a little shake and a twist every day for about a month until the sediment has been gently moved from the side of the bottle into the dome or blister. Leave the bottle completely upside down for a few more days for the sediment to settle.

If a blister stopper has been used, all you have to do is to seal off the blister with the wire provided. The wine is now ready for serving as soon as it is chilled.

If a hollow-domed stopper has been used, the stopper will contain not only the sediment but also a little wine. This can quickly be frozen by chilling the bottle of wine – still upside down – in the refrigerator and then standing the bottle on its stopper in a suitable vessel containing a mixture of crushed ice and kitchen salt. Within eight or ten minutes the stopper will be frozen, the bottle can be stood upright, the cage removed, and the stopper with its ice and sediment eased out. A clean stopper softened in hot water must be quickly inserted and the cage replaced.

It is always as well to chill the wine as much as you can before removing the sediment. If you can get the temperature of the wine down to 2°C (35°F) there will be very little foaming and no wine will be lost.

Proper sparkling wine bottles. No other bottles are suitable and safe

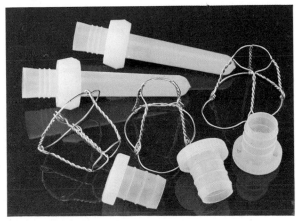

Hollow, plastic stopper, blister stoppers and wire cages

Sweetening the wine

Experience has shown that completely dry sparkling wines are not acceptable to most people. If sugar is added, there is a danger that fermentation may start again. In practice, one saccharin tablet popped into the bottle with the clean stopper takes the edge off the dryness; two make the wine taste semi-sweet and three make it taste quite sweet.

Although the wine is ready for serving as soon as the sediment is removed, it will keep for many months longer. It should be served at a temperature around 8°C (46°F). The cold adds to the freshness of the flavour and slows down the release of the tiny bubbles of carbon dioxide. A tall tulip shaped glass should be used to show the wine off to its best advantage.

Sparkling Apple Wine

3.5 kg (7 lb) eating apples

1.5 kg (3 lb) cooking apples

250 g ($\frac{1}{2}$ lb) concentrated white grape juice

500 g (1 lb) white sugar

2 g ($\frac{1}{2}$ tsp) grape tannin

Pectic enzyme and Campden tablets

1.25 litres (2 pints) water

Champagne wine yeast and nutrient

Remove stalks and wash the apples and, if possible, liquidise them.

Dissolve one Campden tablet and the pectic enzyme in cold boiled water and so arrange that the apple juice flows into the water as it leaves the liquidiser.

Alternatively, place a few apples at a time in a strong plastic bag, crush them finely and empty

Sparkling wine in the process of disgorgement

them into the water. A further alternative is to quarter the apples a few at a time and mince them, arranging for the juice and pulp to fall into the water.

The purpose of all this is to prevent the browning of the fruit through exposure to the air, since this leaves a taint in the wine.

Cover the vessel and leave it in a warm place for 24 hours.

Strain out the pulp through a nylon bag and press it dry. Discard the pulp, stir in the concentrated grape juice and enough sugar to produce a specific gravity of around 1.080.

Add an activated wine yeast, nutrient and tannin, pour the must into a fermentation jar, fit an airlock and ferment out.

Continue as described above.

Sparkling Gooseberry Wine

1 kg (2 lb) green gooseberries ('Careless' variety preferred)

250 g ($\frac{1}{2}$ lb) sultanas

750 g (1$\frac{1}{2}$ lb) white sugar

2 g ($\frac{1}{2}$ tsp) grape tannin

Pectic enzyme and Campden tablets

3.5 litres (7 pints) water

Champagne wine yeast and nutrient

Wash, top and tail the gooseberries, wash and chop the sultanas, place them in a bin and pour hot water over them. Cover and leave to cool. Crush each berry between your fingers, add the pectic enzyme and one crushed Campden tablet, cover and leave for 24 hours.

Add an activated wine yeast, nutrient and tannin and ferment on the pulp for 3 days keeping the fruit submerged and the bin covered.

Strain out and press the pulp dry and discard, stir in the sugar, pour the must into a fermentation jar, fit an airlock and ferment out.

Continue as described above.

Sparkling Rhubarb Wine

2 kg (4 lb) Champagne rhubarb

250 g ($\frac{1}{2}$ lb) sultanas

1 orange

750 g (1$\frac{1}{2}$ lb) white sugar

2 g ($\frac{1}{2}$ tsp) grape tannin

Pectic enzyme and Campden tablets

3 litres (6 pints) water

Champagne wine yeast and nutrient

Top and tail the rhubarb, wipe the stalks with a sulphited cloth and chop into thin slices. Place in a bin containing the water, pectic enzyme and one crushed Campden tablet.

Add the washed and chopped sultanas

and thinly pared rind of the orange and juice previously wiped with a sulphited cloth. Cover the bin and leave it in a warm place for 24 hours.

Add an activated yeast, nutrient and the tannin and ferment on the pulp for 4 days keeping the fruit submerged and the bin covered.

Strain out, press dry and discard the fruit, stir in the sugar, pour the must into a fermentation jar, fit an airlock and ferment out.

Continue as already described.

Sparkling Pear Wine

3 kg (6 lb) hard pears	Pectic enzyme and
250 g (½ lb) sultanas	Campden tablets
750 g (1½ lb) white	3.5 litres (6 pints)
sugar	water
5 g (1 tsp) citric	Champagne wine
acid	yeast and nutrient

Dissolve the acid, pectic enzyme and one crushed Campden tablet in the water.

Wash the pears and mash them finely and add to the water together with the washed and chopped sultanas. Cover and leave for 24 hours.

Add an activated yeast, nutrient and ferment on the pulp for 4 days, keeping the fruit submerged and the bin loosely covered.

Strain out and press the fruit dry, stir in the sugar, pour the must into a fermentation jar, fit an airlock and ferment out.

Continue as already described.

Sparkling Currant Wine

750 g (1½ lb) white	Pectic enzyme and
currants	Campden tablets
500 g (1 lb)	3.5 litres (6 pints)
redcurrants	water
250 g (½ lb)	Champagne wine
blackcurrants	yeast and nutrient
250 g (½ lb) sultanas	
750 g (1½ lb) white	
sugar	

Remove stalks, wash and mash the currants, add the washed and chopped sultanas, place them in a bin containing the water, one crushed Campden tablet and the pectic enzyme. Cover and leave for 24 hours.

Add an activated yeast, nutrient and ferment on the pulp for 3 days, keeping the fruit cap submerged and the bin loosely covered.

Strain out, press dry and discard the fruit, stir in the sugar, pour the must into a fermentation jar, fit an airlock and ferment out.

Continue as already described above.

Because of the high acid content, this sparkling rosé wine is best served medium sweet.

Freezing the neck of a bottle of sparkling wine prior to disgorging the sediment

Removing the frozen stopper containing the sediment

Sparkling Mead

1.25 kg (2½ lb) clover,	3.75 litre (6½ pints)
lime or orange	water
blossom honey	Champagne wine
10 g (2 tsp) citric	yeast and nutrient
acid	
4 g (1 tsp) grape	
tannin	

Dissolve the honey, acid and tannin in warm water and, when cool, check that the specific gravity is around 1.080. If it is lower, stir in a little more honey. If it is higher, dilute with a little more cold boiled water.

Add an activated wine yeast and 2 g (½ tsp) of additional nutrient, pour the must into a fermentation jar, fit an airlock and ferment out to dryness.

Continue as already described.

Dessert wines

These are usually sweet, strong, full-bodied wines served after a meal. The commercial equivalents are port wines, Madeira and cream sherry. Home produced dessert wines must include an increased quantity of appropriate fruits to provide the fuller body required, extra sugar to provide the additional alcohol and the residual sweetness of a dessert wine, and some more acid to maintain the balance. Some additional nutrient including some vitamin B_1 will assist the fermentation to achieve the maximum possible alcohol. The use of multiple ingredients produces a complex bouquet and flavour much more satisfying than can be obtained from a single ingredient. An equal weight of chopped raisins may be used instead of the concentrated grape juice if this is more convenient for you.

To attain the commercial levels of alcohol in your wines you can fortify them with spirit. Vodka, Polish Spirit, or *Eau-de-Vie* is recommended in preference to brandy, gin, rum or whisky. The latter all impart their own particular flavour to the wine, while the former simply re-inforce the natural flavour.

Prolonged fermentation

A high alcohol content can be produced by a prolonged fermentation of the must. In practice this means starting the fermentation in the usual way from an initial specific gravity of around 1.090 – no higher. As the fermentation proceeds, the specific gravity should be checked from time to time and when a reading of 1.010 is reached, some of the must should be removed and enough extra sugar stirred in to raise the reading to 1.030 – no higher. This process must be repeated from time to time until the fermentation stops.

The young wine is then racked from its sediment and sufficient sugar is again stirred in to attain the desired sweetness. It is beneficial not to add all the sugar at the outset since this sometimes inhibits the fermentation. By building up the sugar content at intervals the alcoholic tolerance of the yeast is increased thus enabling it to convert the maximum quantity of sugar to alcohol. By this method it is possible to attain an alcohol content of at least 16% and occasionally even higher. The alcohol content can be calculated by recording every hydrometer reading and adding together the number of units actually fermented.

Demijon and trial jar with hydrometer reading specific gravity

Topping up

For example:		Units fermented
First reading	1.090	
Second reading	1.010 i.e.	80
After sugar added	1.030	
Next reading	1.010 i.e.	20
More sugar added	1.030	
Next reading	1.010 i.e.	20
More sugar added	1.030	
Fermentation stops	1.025 i.e.	5
	Total	125

By reference to the chart on page 31, it will be seen that the complete fermentation of a must with a specific gravity of 1.125 produces 17% alcohol.

This figure can be increased to any desired percentage by fortification with a spirit. Just how much spirit to add can be calculated by reference to a simple formula set out in the form of a square. For example:

```
A              D
        C
B              E
```

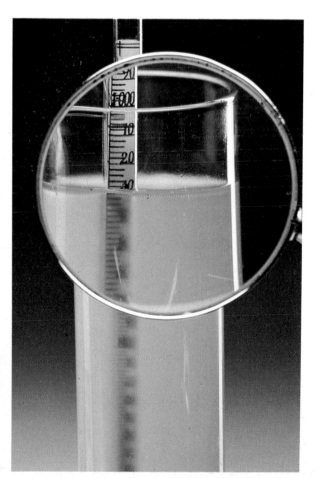

Specific gravity 10.30

At A write the alcohol content of the spirit, say, 40%
At B write the alcohol content of the wine, say, 17%
At C write the alcohol content wanted in the wine, say, 22%
At D write the difference between C and B (22–17) 5
At E write the difference between A and C (40–22) 18

The proportion of D to E is the quantity of spirit at 40% alcohol to add to a wine of 17% alcohol in order to increase the alcohol content of the wine to 22%. That is 5 measures of spirit to 18 measures of wine, or approximately one bottle of spirit to 3 bottles of wine.

Such strong wines need a long period of storage. Two years is a reasonable minimum, but 3 or 4 years may be necessary. It is well worth while waiting for these wines to mature. Give them 2 years' storage in jar and then bottle some of the wine in half-size bottles and the rest in full-size bottles. Four of each is a fair balance. The half size bottles can be opened from time to time at, say, 3 or 4 month intervals to see how the wine is progressing. In this way, there will still be some bottles left when the wine is fully mature. It will keep for at least 10 years and probably much longer before it slowly deteriorates.

Golden Dessert Wine

1 kg (2 lb) old potatoes	1 kg (2 lb) demerara sugar
1 kg (2 lb) raisins	Pectic enzyme and Campden tablets
500 g (1 lb) crushed or flaked malted wheat	4 litres (7 pints) water
500 g (1 lb) cooking apples	Cereal yeast and Madeira wine yeast and nutrient
2 large lemons	
1 Seville orange	

Scrub the potatoes clean and dice them. Wash and chop the raisins, thinly pare the lemons and orange (avoiding all white pith), place all these in a bin and pour hot water over them. Sprinkle on the wheat flakes, cover and leave to cool.

Wash and crush the apples and add to the bin together with the expressed juice of the orange and lemons, the pectic enzyme and one crushed Campden tablet. Cover and leave for 24 hours.

Add an activated cereal yeast and ferment on the pulp for 5 days, keeping the pulp submerged and the bin loosely covered.

Strain out the solids, stir in half the sugar together with an activated Madeira yeast and nutrient. Pour the must into a fermentation jar leaving room for the rest of the sugar, fit an airlock and ferment for 10 days. Stir in half the remaining sugar and 5 days later add the rest.

When fermentation is finished, move the jar to a cool place. Rack the wine into a clean jar, top up with any excess wine. Check the specific gravity and, if necessary add sugar to increase the reading to around 1.020, or sweeten to your taste.

Add one Campden tablet, bung tight, label and store the wine until it is bright, then rack again. Mature this dessert wine for 2 years in bulk and a further year in a bottle before tasting it.

After 3 years try a half bottle and, if necessary, keep the wine for a few months longer, although 3 years is usually long enough. This is a sweet and strong dessert wine, mellow, smooth and of great character. It well repays your trouble and patience.

Red Dessert Wine (1)

2 kg (4 lb) black ripe blackberries	1.5 kg (3 lb) white sugar
500 g (1 lb) black ripe elderberries	10 g (2 tsp) citric acid
1 kg (2 lb) cooking apples	3 g (½ tsp) grape tannin
500 g (1 lb) ripe bananas	Pectic enzyme and Campden tablets
250 g (½ lb) concentrated grape juice (port wine style)	4 litres (7 pints) water
	Port wine yeast and nutrient

Dissolve the citric acid, pectic enzyme and one crushed Campden tablet in the water.

Remove stalks, wash and crush the blackberries and elderberries, peel and mash the bananas, wash and crush the apples and add them all to the water. Cover and leave in a warm place for 24 hours.

Add the concentrated grape juice, tannin, activated yeast and nutrient and ferment on the pulp for 5 days, keeping the pulp well submerged and the bin loosely covered to permit the escape of the gas.

Strain out and press the fruit dry and discard the pulp, stir in half the sugar, pour the must into a fermentation jar leaving some space for the remaining sugar. Fit an airlock and ferment in a warm place for 10 days.

Stir in half the remaining sugar and 5 days later, add the rest.

When fermentation is finished, move the wine to a cool place for a few days, then rack it into a clean jar, topping it up from the excess wine. Add one Campden tablet, bung tight, label and store until the wine is bright. Rack the wine again and store it until it is at least 2

years old, then bottle it and keep it for a further period of at least six months.

This is a smooth, mellow, sweet and strong wine with no dominant flavour of blackberry or elderberry. Serve it free from chill with Stilton cheese.

Red Dessert Wine (2)

2 kg (4 lb) black damsons	1.5 kg (3 lb) white sugar
500 g (1 lb) black-ripe blackberries	10 g (2 tsp) citric acid
500 g (1 lb) cooking apples	5 g (1 tsp) grape tannin
500 g (1 lb) ripe bananas	Pectic enzyme and Campden tablets
250 g (½ lb) dried apricots	4 litres (7 pints) water
250 g (½ lb) concentrated grape juice (port wine style)	Port wine yeast and nutrient

Remove stalks and wash the damsons, wash and chop the apricots, place them in a bin and pour hot water over them. Cover and leave to cool, then crush the damsons and remove the stones.

Add the citric acid, pectic enzyme and one crushed Campden tablet, then add the washed and crushed blackberries, the peeled and mashed bananas and the crushed apples. Replace the cover and leave for 24 hours.

Add the grape concentrate, tannin, activated yeast, nutrient and tannin and ferment on the pulp for 5 days, keeping the pulp submerged.

Strain out, press dry and discard the fruit, stir in half the sugar, pour the must into a fermentation jar, leaving some room for the remaining sugar. Fit an airlock and ferment for 10 days. Add half the remaining sugar and 5 days later add the rest.

When fermentation is finished, move the jar to a cool place for a few days, then rack the wine into a clean jar and add one Campden tablet. Bung tight, label and store for 2 years, then bottle and keep for at least a further 6 months.

Serve this wine free from chill at the end of a meal. It will have an indefinable fruity, vinous bouquet and flavour, and will be smooth, rich and strong.

Red Dessert Wine (3)

1.5 kg (3 lb) black-ripe elderberries	1.5 kg (3 lb) white sugar
500 g (1 lb) cooking apples	10 g (2 tsp) citric acid
500 g (1 lb) ripe bananas	5 g (1 tsp) grape tannin
250 g (½ lb) dried apricots	Pectic enzyme and Campden tablets
250 g (½ lb) concentrated grape juice (port wine style)	4 litres (7 pints) water
	Port wine yeast and nutrient

Dissolve the citric acid, pectic enzyme and one crushed Campden tablet in half the water, then add the washed and crushed apples.

Remove stalks, wash and crush the elderberries, peel and mash the bananas, wash and chop the apricots. Place them all in a boiling pan with the other half of the water. Slowly heat to 80°C (175°F), maintain this temperature for 15 minutes, then leave the fruit to cool. Strain out the solids in a nylon bag, press dry and discard and pour the juice into the bin with the apples. Cover the bin and leave it for 24 hours.

Add the concentrated grape juice, tannin, activated yeast, and nutrient and ferment the apples on the pulp for 5 days, keeping them well submerged and the bin loosely covered or fitted with an airlock.

Strain out and press the apples dry and discard the pulp. Stir in half the sugar and pour the must into a fermentation jar leaving some room for the rest of the sugar. Fit an airlock and ferment for 10 days. Add half the remaining sugar and 5 days later the rest.

When fermentation is finished, move the wine to a cool place for a few days, then rack it into a clean jar and top up from the excess. Add one Campden tablet, bung tight, label and store until bright, then rack again and store for 2 years before bottling. Keep for a further year if possible.

Because of the extremely heavy tax on them, genuine liqueurs are very expensive. Successful alternatives can be made in the home, however, for around one-third of the cost. A wide range of flavours are marketed, the best of which come from France. In addition to the liqueur essence, you need some spirit, some strong wine and some sugar. A little glycerine and oil of capsicum add a richness and warmth to the liqueur.

So as not to alter the appearance and flavour of the essence, the colourless and tasteless spirit, vodka, is mostly used. The French 'Eau-de-vie pour les fruits' is also suitable and the colourless Bacardi may be used for the coffee rum liqueur. Ordinary brandy, rum and whisky are not suitable because they change the flavour too much. Gin is only suitable with damsons, sloes and orange peel.

A strong bland white wine is required for most liqueurs, although a good red one is needed for the 'cherry brandy'. If the wine is sweet, then less sugar is needed. A wine made from concentrated grape juice is perfectly suitable as this usually lacks distinctive flavouring. Caster sugar dissolves more easily than granulated sugar, but either may be used.

The phials of essence are enough to make one litre of liqueur, so, if you make only a standard bottle – 750 ml (26⅔ fl oz) – you need only use three-quarters of the essence.

For a litre bottle:	For a standard wine bottle:
20 ml essence	3 tsp essence
340 g sugar	9 oz sugar
340 ml vodka	9 fl oz vodka
450 ml wine	12 fl oz wine
20 ml glycerine	3 tsp glycerine
16 drops capsicum tincture (available at most chemists)	12 drops capsicum tincture (available) at most chemists)

Mix all the ingredients together until the sugar is completely dissolved. Do this by stirring gently and do not heat so as not to dissipate the esters and alcohol. The liqueur is ready to serve immediately, although it improves slightly if left for a few days to homogenise. If the wine is sweet, it is best to use only two-thirds of the sugar at first and to add more as may be thought necessary.

Assuming that a vodka of 40% alcohol is used and that the strong wine contains 16% alcohol, the resultant liqueur will contain nearly 22% alcohol. The glycerine and capsicum tincture will give the impression of an even greater strength. Many genuine liqueurs are not much stronger. Cherry Brandy and Peach Brandy are about 24% alcohol; Apricot Brandy and Crême de

Menthe are about 28% alcohol and Tia Maria is about 31%.

A litre bottle of vodka is enough to make either four bottles or three litres of the liqueurs mentioned, but you may increase the quantity of vodka used and decrease the quantity of wine if you so wish. It is worth making three or four different liqueurs at a time so that you have a choice to offer your friends. There are many brands of essences on sale, but much experience has shown the French essences to produce liqueurs nearest in flavour to the original liqueur. They can be obtained from most Home Brew shops and are worth searching for.

The French 'Eau-de-vie·pour les fruits'

Mix the ingredients together

Basic ingredients.
Strong sweet wine, vodka and sugar

already mentioned, is not readily available in the United Kingdom, although it is on sale in almost every wine shop in France. It is a simple distillation of wine made from no particular grape variety, whereas brandy is made from selected grape varieties especially suitable for the purpose and is matured in oak for 3 years before it is flavoured with caramel.

In France, *eau-de-vie* is used for marinading fruits and this is another way of making liqueurs in the home. Select only the very best quality fruits, wash and drain them, or stone and peel them as necessary. Prick the soft fruit with a bodkin or fork and slice the stoned fruit, place them in a wide mouthed jar, sprinkle on 2 tablespoonfuls caster sugar and cover them with *eau-de-vie*. Seal the jar and store it in a dark place. Shake it daily until all the sugar is dissolved, then occasionally to dissipate the fruit flavour into the *eau-de-vie*. After 3 months, strain off the liqueur into an appropriately sized bottle and eat the fruit as a luxury dessert. Both are scrumptious!

The same method is used for making sloe gin. Choose very ripe, soft, black sloes, wash them, remove the stalks and drain them. Prick them all over with a bodkin or fork so that the juice can get out, place them in a wide mouthed jar, sprinkle them with sugar and cover them with gin. Continue as above. For one bottle of gin you need at least 350 g (12 oz) sloes and 175 g (6 oz) sugar, but you may use up to 500 g (1 lb) sloes and 250 g ($\frac{1}{2}$ lb) sugar for one litre.

Orange gin is made by steeping the thinly pared and chopped rind of one Seville orange and one lemon in a bottle of gin that has been sweetened with 250 g (8 oz) sugar. Remove the fruit parings after one week. Both liqueurs are improved with a large teaspoonful of glycerine.

Liqueurs made by the marinading of fresh fruits need some months, at least, to mature after the removal of the fruit. Indeed, a year or more may be required for the harshness of the sloe to mellow, depending on its original condition and ripeness.

Black-ripe damsons may be used instead of sloes. After removing the stalks and washing them, cut them in two and remove the stones. A poor man's cherry brandy can be made with ripe morello cherries and strong ale. It is a surprisingly well flavoured and satisfying beverage that was once very popular in Kent.

500 g (1 lb) black ripe morello cherries	500 g (1 lb) demerara sugar
2 litres (3 pints) strong ale	Wine yeast and nutrient

Remove stalks, wash and prick the cherries with a bodkin or fork, place them in a wide mouthed jar, cover them with the sugar and slowly pour on the beer so as not to create too much froth. A large sweet jar is suitable. Give the fruit a good stir up, but gently, then sprinkle on a sachet of wine yeast and nutrient. Cover the jar with a sheet of polythene, tied with wool so that the gas can escape. Ferment in a warm place and when fermentation is finished, move the jar to a cool place while the 'brandy' clears. When it is bright, siphon it into bottles, seal and store these for a few months. Serve the cherries in an open flan topped with cream; they are delicious, too.

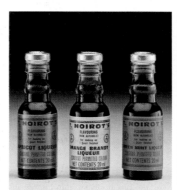 

(left) Assorted liqueur flavourings
(right) Flavouring, glycerine and capsicum tincture

Fine large prunes with Eau-de-Vie

Choice large prunes, washed and pricked, then covered with a strong, sweet white wine and left for 3 months, except for an occasional shake, produce both a rich, liqueur-like drink and a delicious dessert. Selected dried apricot halves are equally good, but the fruit must be of the finest quality or the result can be disappointing.

Home produced liqueurs may be served in exactly the same way as their more expensive originals. Enjoy them after a meal, poured over ice cream, added to fruit desserts or use them in cooking.

SERVING WINE

Your wine can be enhanced by the manner in which you serve it. Taking care to select the right wine for the right occasions and serving it in the right manner, ensures that your trouble and patience is well rewarded.

Do try to let your wines mature adequately. Far too many wines are drunk too young and, all too often, the best bottle is the last. Some wines are ready for drinking within 3 or 4 months, whilst others take almost as many years to mature. Taste your wines from time to time and put back for further storage those that are not ready for drinking.

When you deem that they are ready, select from your range the most suitable for the purpose or the occasion. Try not to drink your wines indiscriminately. Select the most suitable for an aperitif, a dry white wine for fish, pork or poultry, a dry red table wine for red meats and game, a sweet white wine for the dessert course, a strong sweet wine or liqueur for the end of the meal, a sparkling wine to celebrate some especially happy occasion.

Consider, too, the company with whom you will share the wine. Do they appreciate and enjoy wine or would they rather drink beer or water? Do they prefer only sweet wines with everything? Whilst you may not agree with their choice, respect their tastes while they are your guests and do not waste your best wines on them. But to those wine-lovers like yourself, serve your very best wines. Their pleasure will increase your pleasure and the wine will taste even better. There is an old dictum, 'Serve your best wines to your best friends on your best occasions and drink your lesser wines with your family every day.' It makes more sense than you might at first think.

Having selected your wine, prepare it for table. Bring a red wine into a warm room for the best part of a day so that it can slowly lose its chill. Never stand cold red wines on boilers

Decanters of wine on a silver tray

or radiators or in buckets of hot water to warm them up quickly. They resent such indignities and do not give their best bouquet and flavour. In any case they do not need to be warm but only free from chill. A temperature around 19–20°C (66–68°F) is about right. Treat them with gentle care and they will repay your efforts.

White wines, on the other hand, like to be nicely chilled. They can be stood in the refrigerator (never the freezer) for an hour or so to acquire a temperature around 14–15°C (48–50°F). Rosé wines are at their best a degree or two higher and sparkling wines just a few degrees lower. A bucket containing water and ice cubes may also be used.

This matter of temperature is much more important than is generally believed. Try drinking a really cold, dry elderberry wine; it makes your hair stand on end! An unchilled white wine tastes dull, soft and flabby!

Nearly all home-made wines benefit from a period in a decanter – even half an hour helps

Glasses for different wines (left to right) Bordeaux goblet and Paris goblet for red wines, tulip for white wines, liqueur glass, copita for sherry-style wines, flute for sparkling wines

remains cool. Red wines are served in more spherical shaped bowls for the opposite reason. Sparkling wines are served in tall flutes so that the tiny bubbles of delight have further to rise and so increase our enjoyment. Liqueurs are served in small glasses because of their strength and cloying sweetness.

All glasses should be plain and free from distracting embellishments of any kind. Coloured glasses were only used in the past to mask the haziness then so prevalent. Heavily cut, engraved and decorated glasses all distract one's attention from the beautiful colour and clarity of the wine.

If possible, glasses and decanters should be stood on silver salvers so that the hue of the wine is reflected and emphasised. If a salver is not available, a plain white linen cloth is the next best. At all events, avoid coloured trays or cloths which tend to camouflage the wine.

Use your wine in preparing your food, too. Marinade fish and meat in dry wine, especially the coarser grained fish and cuts of meat. The wine tenderises them and enhances the flavour. Use wine instead of water when stewing fruit, pour sweet white wines over fresh fruits and fruit salads. Add wine to casseroles, meat pies and stews. Use it sparingly so that the taste of the wine is barely noticeable, if at all. There is no need to use your best wine since the ends of bottles collected together do just as well.

Pick a glass up by its stem, hold it by the base with your thumb on top and your fingers beneath. Never touch the bowl so as not to vary the temperature nor mar the polished surface with finger and thumb prints. Smell the bouquet and consider its clean freshness, its fruitiness, its vinosity and its depth of fragrance. Take a mouthful of wine, chew it and move it around your cheeks, your tongue and your gums before swallowing it. Pause to savour the complexity of taste, wait for the aftertaste or farewell to develop and enjoy this last moment of delight. Then mark your wine in your mind:

	Colour and clarity	Bouquet	Taste and general impression
Superb	4	4	12–10
Very good	3	3	9–7
Good	2	2	6–4
Fair	1	1	3–1
Poor	0	0	0

Not every wine will be superb, although some will. But many will vary from Very Good to Good and only occasionally will you need to grade one as Fair. If you have taken proper care, none need ever be Poor. It is often said that there are no bad wines; just that some are better than others.

a still-young wine to improve. Reds benefit from a little longer than whites. The larger surface exposed to the air in a decanter enables the bouquet and flavour of a wine to develop and improve. Furthermore, the wine looks so much better in a colourless, glass decanter. The colour and clarity of a wine become instantly appealing in a decanter. Served in the green glass bottle in which it was stored, one can see only the label – often hand written and smudged.

The glasses in which your wines are served are also important if you want to enjoy them to the full. All glasses should consist of an incurved bowl on a stem connected to a base. The stem lifts the bowl up so that it can be clearly seen above the cutlery, crockery and nappery of the table. The incurve of the bowl retains the bouquet for your enjoyment. Aperitifs and dessert wines, being stronger, are served in smaller glasses than table wines. White table wines are served in tulip shaped glasses so that less wine is exposed at the surface and it

A selection of wet kits

Beer kits

The most popular way of brewing beer at home is from kits. They are available in all the standard beer styles: Bitter, Brown Ale, Mild, Stout, Lager, Barley Wine. Some manufacturers even include Shandy, Light Ale and Northern Brown in their range.

Kits enable you to brew your favourite beer with the minimum of equipment and by the simplest of methods. Manufacturers claim that the beer made from their kits is ready for drinking within 10 days of starting the brew. This is the absolute minimum, however, and experience shows that the quality improves if the beer is allowed to mature for another week or two.

Wet kits

There are two types of kits, known in the trade as the wet and the dry. The wet kit consists of a quantity of a very thick malt syrup containing hop essences. The manufacturer mashes the appropriate blend of malted barley and adjuncts, boils this wort with the right variety and quantity of hops for the style and then evaporates about 80% of the water. The heavy brown syrup that results looks very much like toffee in the making. It is packed in cans or strong, heat-sealed, plastic bags and marketed in various sizes sufficient to produce 16, 24, 32 or 40 pints of beer. A sachet of yeast granules and usually one of beer finings is

John Bull and Unican wet kits

Beer making equipment

A selection of dry kits

enclosed in the pack together with detailed instructions, often with line drawings, to show you how to brew that beer. All that you have to provide is some sugar and water.

Dry kits

The dry kit consists of a carton containing a muslin bag of hops and crushed malt grains, a sealed plastic bag of dry malt flour and another of dried yeast granules. Some locally produced kits even contain a bag of glucose powder. Detailed instructions are provided with each kit. Although the method is slightly more messy, the result is claimed to be a better tasting beer containing the tang of freshly boiled hops. Only water and, usually, sugar have to be supplied by the home brewer.

These kits, too, are available in a range of different styles, notably Lager, Bitter, Brown Ale and Stout and are marketed in different sizes to produce 16, 24, 32 or 40 pints of beer.

Unlike the wet kits which are produced by major companies and distributed nation wide, the dry kits are also produced by some local Home Brew Suppliers, for sale only in their own shops. Often, only a single style is available, possibly taking account of the mineral content of the local water supply. Some local kits have been highly praised in spite of being more expensive than the nationally available dry kits. The cost per pint of kit beer varies from 10 to 20% of its commercial equivalent.

Check the temperature

Add the yeast

Fermentation in progress

Fermentation finished

Brewing from kits

Equipment
Depending on the quality of beer being brewed, a polythene bin is required of a size to hold the brew and leave some head space. It should be provided with a loose fitting lid.

A long handled spoon is needed for stirring the wort and a length of plastic or rubber tubing is needed for siphoning the finished beer into bottles. Enough bottles, with matching screw stoppers or crown caps, sufficient for the quantity of beer are needed. They should be strong beer bottles and *not* non-returnable bottles. If crown caps are to be used, a capping tool will be required.

Some kits contain printed coloured labels, but these may be bought separately. They contribute a 'professional' finish to the bottle.

A large stew pan or preserving pan is needed for boiling the ingredients of dry kits and even some wet kits.

A measuring jug is needed to ensure that neither too much nor too little water is used.

Cleanliness
It is essential that all the equipment, bin, spoon, siphon, bottles, stoppers, jug and pan, is clean and sterile. Two Campden tablets and a half teaspoonful of citric acid dissolved in one pint of cold water make a satisfactory sterilising solution for clean equipment. A suitable sterilising detergent can be bought for cleaning dirty bottles. Rinse each piece of equipment with the Campden solution and shake off the surplus drops immediately prior to use.

Method for wet kits
Open the container and pour the contents into the sterilised brewing bin or boiling pan as directed by the instructions.

Pour on the specified quantity of hot water, rinse out the container and stir well until the malt extract is dissolved.

If the extract solution has to be boiled, simmer it gently for five minutes. One kit recommends the addition of gelatine finings at this stage.

Pour the wort into the brewing bin, stir in the required amount of sugar, if any, stir well and then add the right amount of water.

Check the temperature of the wort and provided it is within the range 18 to 24°C (65 to 75°F), sprinkle the contents of the yeast sachet onto the surface.

Cover the vessel and leave the brew to ferment in an area where the temperature range just mentioned can be maintained. The cover should protect the brew from dust and dirt but loose enough for the carbon dioxide generated by the fermentation to escape.

The instructions with some kits recommends skimming off the frothy yeast head and rousing up the beer on the second and third days. With other kits this is not necessary.

Fermentation will take from five to seven days depending on the strength of the brew and the warmth of its position.

Fermentation is complete when the bubbles stop rising and the surface clears. It can be checked with an hydrometer. If the reading remains stationery for two days at a reading of 1.006 or below, fermentation is finished.

Move the bin to a cool place for another day or so while the beer clears.

Lift the bin onto a table without disturbing the sediment and siphon the clearing beer into the sterilising bottles. By careful positioning of the tube in the bin and by carefully tilting the bin as it is emptied, nearly all the beer can be removed without carrying over any of the thick yeast paste on the bottom of the bin.

Fill each bottle to within 4 cm (1½ in) of the top, leaving this space for pressure to build up from the bottle fermentation.

Add only half a level teaspoonful of sugar to each one pint of beer and seal the bottles immediately.

Shake the bottles gently to dissolve the sugar and to test the seal. If the bottle hisses the seal is imperfect and should be rectified.

Label the bottles with their style and date and leave them in a warm room for a few days while the sugar is fermented.

Move the bottles to a cool store for a week or two while the beer matures.

Method for dry kits

Open the carton, check the contents and place the muslin bag and its contents in a large pan. Pour on the quantity of water recommended, place the pan on a stove and boil it vigorously for 45 minutes. The pan should be covered to minimise evaporation and the loss of aroma.

Empty the malt flour into a brewing bin, mix in the sugar, pour on some hot water, a little at first, and stir until a smooth paste is made. Add more hot water to thin the paste until the recommended quantity has been added. This method prevents the flour from lumping and ensures complete dissolution.

Lift out and drain the bag of hops and grains. Pour the liquor into the brewing bin, stir well, then top up with cold water.

Check the temperature of the brew and when it is within the range 18 to 24°C (65 to 75°F), sprinkle the contents of the yeast bag onto the surface of the wort. Cover the bin loosely and leave it in a warm place.

On the second and third days skim off the dirty froth and stir the beer thoroughly.

Continue as already described for wet kits.

Draught beers

Beer made from both wet and dry kits may be casked instead of bottled. When the beer is finished, instead of siphoning it into bottles, sterilise a plastic pressure cask and siphon the beer into that. Dissolve 56 g (2 oz) sugar in a little cold water and mix it into 22.5 litres (5 gallons) of beer. Screw the lid onto the cask making sure that you have secured a perfect fit.

Leave the cask for a week or ten days before serving the beer. This gives time for the sugar to be fermented and for the beer to clear and mature. The first half of the brew can be drawn off in good condition and with plenty of life.

When the liveliness diminishes, the beer must either be re-primed with 28 g (1 oz) sugar or some carbon dioxide from an injector bulb fitted to the lid, must be released into the cask.

Draught beers are rarely quite as bright as bottled beers, but this disadvantage is more than offset by the saving in time and effort in not having to sterilise, fill, prime, seal and store forty bottles of beer – quite a chore on your own!

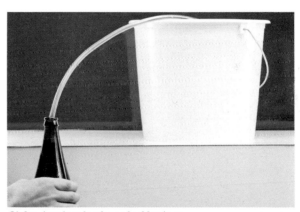

Siphon into beer bottles and add primer

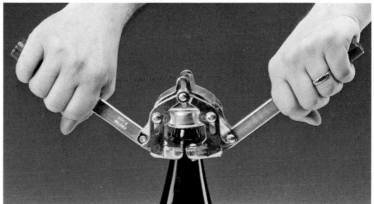

Bottling technique

From malt extract and hops

Having mastered the craft of brewing beer from kits, many people develop the desire to brew something a little different, something in which their judgement has played some part in its creation. The logical step is to brew from a straight malt extract flavoured with freshly boiled hops.

Extracts

As with the kits, there is a choice of extracts, both wet and dry. Home Brew shops and some garden centres and chemists offer a selection of the toffee-like malt extracts appropriate for brewing lagers, bitters and stouts. Also available is a choice of pale, medium or dark malt flour.

Hops

A choice of hops is available too. The Golding-types suitable for light ales and bitter beers; the Fuggle-types suitable for brown ales and stouts; and, in some places, Continental hops for use in brewing lager-type beers.

Yeast

There is even a choice of yeast – an ale yeast for ales and bitter beers and a stout yeast for stouts.

Hops as they grow on the bine

For the lager brewer, a Continental lager yeast can be bought. It ferments differently from English yeast, working at a lower temperature and from the bottom of the brew.

Water

The kind of water available from the tap becomes significant, too. A hard water has long been proved best for bitter beers, while brown ales and stouts taste better with a softer water. Mineral salts can be bought to add to soft water to make it hard. They are usually sold in small packets and are called 'hardening salts'. Hard water can be softened by the addition of some ordinary table or cooking salt.

Equipment

No additional equipment is necessary, apart from a suitable pan in which to boil the hops. A large stew pan will do, or a preserving pan. If you don't like the smell of boiling hops you can use a pressure cooker.

Basic recipe

A wide range of choices are now available to you. A basic recipe is as follows:

Bitter Beer

Recommended original gravity 1.038–1.042.

1 kg (2 lb) malt extract	10 litres (2 gallons) water
500 g (1 lb) white sugar	Ale yeast
60 g (2 oz) Golding type hops	

Dissolve the malt extract in some warm water in a polythene bin and rinse out the container to make sure that none is wasted.

Stir in the sugar until it is dissolved and add any hardening salts that may be necessary.

Boil the hops vigorously for 45 minutes, leave them to cool and settle for a short while, then strain the liquor into the malt and sugar solution.

Top up to the 10 litres (2 gallons) level with cold water and check the temperature. When the reading is between 18–20°C (64 and 68°F) pitch an ale yeast that has been activated in 250 ml ($\frac{1}{2}$ pint) of a weak malt solution.

Cover the bin to keep out the dust but not so tight as to restrict the escape of the gas, and leave the wort to ferment for about five days. On the second and third days, skim off the froth and wipe away the yeast ring around the bin at the surface of the wort.

When fermentation is finished a ring of bubbles will collect in the centre of the surface and then disappear.

Move the beer to a cool place for a day or two or rack it at once into fermentation jars and fit

Dissolve the malt extract in a brewing bin

A bag of hops from a dry kit

in the extract. The hops may then be washed with a little warm water to remove the final traces of malt.

Keep back a handful of hops and add to the fermenting wort after the third day when skimming is finished. This adds a fresh hop aroma to the beer.

Use 45 g (1½ oz) 'Golding' hops and 15 g (½ oz) 'Northern Brewer' hops. Add the latter only 15 minutes before the end of the boiling. This improves the tang of the hop flavour.

Try one of the new hop varieties such as 'Wye Challenger' but use only a total of 45 g (1½ oz) since these have a stronger flavour than 'Goldings'.

Sugars for beermaking

Marginally increase or decrease the amount of malt extract used to vary the malty taste of the beer, say, by 125 g (4 oz).

Marginally increase or decrease the total quantity of hops used to vary the bitterness of the beer, say, by 7.5 g (¼ oz).

Marginally increase or decrease the amount of sugar used to vary the alcoholic content of the beer, say, by 125 g (4 oz).

Use a pale malt flour instead of the malt extract syrup. Since the malt flour contains no water 750 g (1½ lb) will be sufficient, but the quantity can be varied slightly.

Vary the flavour and body by adding 125 g (4 oz) flaked maize or flaked wheat. The latter can be bought in supermarkets everywhere as a breakfast cereal.

Instead of bottling the beer, siphon it into a cask 10 litres (2 gallons), prime it with 45 g (1½ oz) sugar dissolved in some of the beer and serve it as draught bitter, after 2 weeks storage.

Different styles
All the different styles of beer can be made just as easily and all with your own individual touch. The recipes that follow are meant to give you not only a formula for a well proved beer, but also ideas on which you can experiment with your own variations.

airlocks. Within a few days the beer will throw a heavy sediment of yeast paste and will be ready for bottling.

The bottling and priming procedure is exactly the same as already described for kit beers. Store the beer for 3 or 4 weeks in a cool place while it matures and develops condition.

Variations
From this basic method there are many individual variations. For example:
Boil the malt extract with the hops and leave the brew for half an hour before straining out the hops. This helps to precipitate any solids

Two other kinds of malt extract syrup are also available to help you. One is called DMS which stands for diastatic malt syrup. This malt extract has been so prepared as to retain a quantity of the enzyme called diastase which converts starch to sugar. It is particularly useful when you intend to add other starch material to your brew, such as flaked maize, rice or wheat. The extra enzymes convert the unfermentable added starch into fermentable sugar, thus increasing the alcoholic content of the beer. It is a little more expensive but it can be used in place of some rather than all of the malt extract – say a quarter to a third. The unused quantity may be sealed with a polythene lid and safely stored in the refrigerator for several months.

The other variety is called SFX which stands for superflavex and is made from selected choice malted barleys. It is worth trying, to see whether you enjoy the flavour.

Mild Ale

Recommended original gravity 1.026 – 1.030.

500 g (1 lb) SFX malt syrup	5 litres (1 gallon) water
15 g ($\frac{1}{2}$ oz) hops of your choice	Ale yeast

Brew beer as above. The result is a not too strong, not too bitter, but malty flavoured beer.

The quantity can be increased to fill a cask so that the beer can be served as a draught rather than a bottled beer.

By way of variation use either a pale or a medium malt flour instead of the syrup.

Alternatively brew 10 litres (2 gallons) by using 500 g (1 lb) SFX malt syrup and 500 g (1 lb) pale or medium malt flour.

Even this can be varied by mixing the pale and medium flours together.

These variations adjust the colour as well as the flavour.

Don't forget to double the hops if you double the quantity of malt and water.

Brown Ale

Recommended original gravity 1.030–1.034.

500 g (1 lb) medium malt flour	21 g ($\frac{3}{4}$ oz) 'Fuggle' type hops
60 g (2 oz) black malt grains	5 litres (1 gallon) water
125 g (4 oz) brown sugar	Ale yeast

Boil the black malt grains with the hops but otherwise brew this beer as above.

If your tap water is hard, add one half teaspoonful of table salt to the brew.

A slightly sweeter or less dry beer can be made by adding 90 g (3 oz) of lactose, an unfermentable sugar only one-third as sweet as household sugar, just prior to bottling.

Mugs and glasses for beer

Stout

Recommended original gravity 1.038–1.042.

500 g (1 lb) dark malt flour or stout-style malt syrup	30 g (1 oz) 'Fuggle' type hops
125 g (4 oz) black malt grains	5 litres (1 gallon) water
250 g (½ lb) dark brown sugar	Stout yeast

Make in the same way as brown ale. Soft water is preferred so add salt if your water is hard.

Sweeten to taste if you wish with lactose – you may need 135 g (4½ oz).

As a variation, try the new 'Wye Northdown' hops in place of the 'Fuggles'. They are much more bitter so use only one-half to three-quarters of the quantity.

A fuller stout can be made by boiling a dark DMS with 60 g (2 oz) of flaked rice or a brewing flour with the malt and hops.

The black malt grains add only colour and flavour to stouts and brown ales.

Strong Ale

Recommended original gravity 1.046–1.050.

500 g (1 lb) SFX malt syrup	30 g (1 oz) 'Wye Challenger' hops
250 g (½ lb) pale malt flour	5 litres (1 gallon) water
250 g (½ lb) light brown sugar	Ale yeast

Hard water is preferred so include some hardening salts if you live in a soft to medium hard water area. The quantity will be given on the packet.

Brew the beer as already described for the basic beer. This is a beer worth 'dry hopping', i.e. saving a few of the hops to add to the fermenting wort after the skimming. Alternatively, a few hop pellets could be used.

This beer must be stored for at least six weeks and will keep for more than a year.

Lager

Recommended original gravity 1.038–1.042.

500 g (1 lb) DMS	5 litres (1 gallon) water
60 g (2 oz) flaked rice	Continental lager yeast (Carlsbergensis)
250 g (½ lb) glucose	
5 g (1 tsp) citric acid	
15 g (½ oz) 'Hallertau' hops	

Soft water is needed for lager so add 3 g (½ tsp) table salt in medium to hard water areas.

Dissolve the malt, acid (and salt) in warm water, add the hops and flaked rice and boil it for half an hour under a lid. Leave it for a short while, then strain out the hops and rice and rinse them free of malt syrup.

Stir in the glucose, top up with cold water and adjust the specific gravity.

When the wort is cold, stir in an activated lager yeast. Pour the wort into a fermentation jar, fit an airlock and leave the jar in a cool place to ferment out – a period of several weeks depending on the temperature – around 10°C (50°F) is desirable.

When fermentation is finished, rack, bottle, prime, seal and store for at least 3 months. Serve this beer cool.

Barley Wine

Recommended original specific gravity 1.078–1.082.

1 kg (2 lb) SFX malt syrup	30 g (1 oz) 'Wye Challenger' or 'Golding' hops
500 g (1 lb) Demerara sugar	
5 g (1 tsp) citric acid	5 litres (1 gallon) water
3 g (½ tsp) nutrient salts	Ale and Champagne wine yeasts

Hard water is needed so adjust as necessary. Make up as basic recipe, but after skimming, rack into a fermentation jar, add an activated Champagne wine yeast and nutrient, fit an airlock and ferment out. Rack, bottle, prime, seal and store for 6 to 12 months.

From grains and adjuncts

When brewing beer from kits, all the preparatory work is done for you by the manufacturer. When brewing beer from malt extract and hops, the manufacturer supplies you with a prepared malt solution. When brewing beer from grains and adjuncts you have to do everything except malt the grains of barley.

The process of mashing grains, however, is not much more difficult than mashing a pot of tea, but it does take time and does need attention. The lovers of really good beer declare that the very best beer can only be made from freshly mashed grains.

Equipment

A suitable vessel in which to mash the grains is essential. One fitted with a variable thermostat is highly desirable.

A boiling pan is also needed and this facility can be built into certain mashing vessels.

It is also helpful if the mashing vessel is fitted with a stainless steel grid or sieve and a draw-off tap. This too is sometimes fitted to mashing vessels. If not a wide necked straining bag is also needed.

A thermometer is essential when mashing grains since the correct temperature at all times is most important.

A hydrometer, too, is essential for producing beer of the right strength for the style.

A facility for spraying the grains with water to rinse out the last remnants of malt sugar is also desirable.

Ingredients

1. *Malt* Malted barley grains are the basic ingredient. They come in various colours depending on how long they have been roasted. Pale malt is most used, although some crystal malt is often added to deepen the colour of a beer. Both will produce about 70% of their weight as a fermentable sugar.

The darker malts, chocolate and black, are used to give colour and flavour to beers especially to brown ales and stouts.

After the grains have been malted they have to be cracked or crushed so that access can be obtained to the starch within. It is best to buy grains that are already crushed, as long as they are fresh. If you have to crush them yourself use a coarse mincer or roll a few at a time with a bottle or ceramic rolling pin on a formica-type surface. It is important not to grind them too fine, in case the mash turns into a porridge!

Malted grains are best used when fresh, since they soon pick up moisture from the air and deteriorate. If you buy more than

(left to right) Crushed pale malt, chocolate malt, crystal malt

you need for one brew, keep the surplus in a brown paper bag inside an airtight container, stored in a cool, dry place.

2. *Hops* The hops, too, should be as fresh as possible. Browning or stale looking hops should be avoided. Always buy the best even if it means a few coppers more. Any saving from buying inferior hops (or malt) is infinitesimal when spread over the brew, but the poorer quality of the beer is noticeable.

There are new varieties of hops available now – notably 'Wye Challenger' for bitter beers and 'Wye Northdown' for stouts. They contain more bittering substance than the 'Goldings' and 'Fuggles' that have been in use for the past century, so use fewer of them. Hop pellets are also available. These consist of ground up hops compressed into pellets. Some of these are twice as strong as the fresh hops, so fewer are required.

3. *Adjuncts* These consist of a variety of ingredients added to replace some of the more expensive barley and to enhance the flavour.

(back row) Glucose chips, brown sugar, demerera flaked maize
(front row) Brewing flour, white sugar and flakes of rice
(foreground) Brewing yeast

Your Home Brew shop will have a selection. Use them sparingly and never let the quantity of adjuncts exceed 20% of the malt. It is customary to add them to the grains at the start of mashing. Adjuncts include torrified barley, roasted barley, flaked maize, rice and wheat, *brewing* flour and, of course, sugar in its various forms.

4. *Sugar* At this level of brewing the enthusiast uses invert sugar rather than household sugar. Household sugar is a combination of 2 simple sugars – glucose and fructose. Before yeast can ferment household sugar, one of its enzymes has to split it into the 2 simple sugars. Invert sugar consists of a mixture of these 2 simple sugars and so is immediately fermentable. For this reason some home brewers use glucose powder or glucose chips instead of household sugar. When available in Home Brew shops invert sugar is quite expensive and contains 25% water. It can easily be made in the home just by boiling household sugar with a little citric acid in water for 20 minutes. Leave the syrup to cool and stir it in when required. 2 lb sugar plus 1 tsp citric acid boiled in 1 pint water produces 2 pints invert sugar syrup. 1 kg sugar plus 5 g citric acid boiled in 380 mls water produces 1 litre invert sugar syrup.

Golden syrup, black treacle and honey may be used as well as brown sugars. They all add flavour to the beer.

Mashing

This process is no more than the soaking of the grains and adjuncts in suitably hard, or soft, hot water – from one-half to two-thirds of the total quantity – until all the starch has been converted to maltose, the name of the sugar that is fermented into beer. At certain temperatures an enzyme in the grain (called diastase) converts more of the starch to maltose, at others, an almost unfermentable sugar called dextrin is also released. Depending on the style of beer required, then, the brewer adjusts the temperature of the mash towards 60°C (140°F) for more maltose, and towards 70°C (158°F) when some dextrin is also required. Dextrin gives a beer body and mitigates a too dry flavour. A full bodied beer with a certain sweetness in the finish should therefore be mashed at a higher temperature than a light ale in which little body and no sweetness is required.

In practice, the malt grains and adjuncts are mostly mashed at 66.5°C (152°F) or just below. The mashing process takes several hours and the temperature must be maintained as steadily as possible the whole time. The mashing vessel may be lagged to conserve the heat but the temperature should be checked and heat applied if necessary every 15 minutes or so, after stirring the mash.

End point

When two hours have elapsed a tablespoonful of the malt solution must be removed and placed in a white saucer. Into this place two or three drops of ordinary household tincture of iodine. If the colour darkens or turns blue, then starch remains in the mash and the temperature must be maintained. Repeat the experiment every half hour until the colour of the solution remains unchanged. This means that all of the starch has been converted into maltose and dextrin.

Sparging

If the vessel in which the grains are soaked has a tap, open it and drain the liquor, now called wort, into a boiling pan. Remove the vessel's lid and spray some hot, not boiling, water over the grains to remove the final traces of sugar. If it is not possible to sparge the grains in this manner, empty the contents of the vessel into a suitable straining bag supported over a boiling pan. Spray the hot water over the grains in the bag. Finally, discard the grains.

Boiling

Now press in the hops, making sure that they are thoroughly wetted and not left floating on the surface. Place the pan on the stove and boil the wort and hops vigorously for up to an hour. Some enthusiasts add a small quantity of Irish moss finings at this stage to ensure a clear wort for the fermentation, but it is not essential. At the end of the boiling, leave the vessel covered for half an hour while the hops

and any sediment settle. Strain off into a fermentation vessel, stir in the sugar, top up with cold water and, when the temperature is down to 16–18°C (61–65°F), check the specific gravity and adjust it as necessary with more sugar or water.

Fermentation, etc.

The process is now the same as for a kit beer, for you have made your own hopped malt solution. Continue as described on page 71.

Light Ale

Recommended original gravity 1.030–1.034 20 litres (4 gallons).

2.5 kg (5 lb) pale malt grains
250 g (½ lb) crystal malt grain
20 litres (4 gallons) hard water
75 g (2½ oz) 'Challenger' hops
Ale yeast

Mash at 65°C (149°F) then boil, cool, adjust specific gravity, yeast, ferment, skim, rack, bottle, prime, seal and store for one month.

Variations

1. Replace one-fifth of the malt grains with 375 g (¾ lb) glucose chips.
2. Replace the crystal malt grains with 180 g (6 oz) brown sugar.
3. Add 250 g (½ lb) flaked maize to the grains.

Bitter

Recommended original gravity 1.038–1.042 20 litres (4 gallons).

2 kg (4 lb) pale malt grains
500 g (1 lb) crystal malt grains
250 g (½ lb) flaked maize
250 g (½ lb) flaked rice
90 g (3 oz) 'Challenger' or 'Golding' hops
15 g (½ oz) 'Northern Brewer' hops
20 litres (4 gallons) hard water
Irish moss
Ale yeast
Glucose powder if necessary

Mash at 66.5°C (152°F). Boil with the 'Challenger' or 'Golding' hops and add 'Northern Brewer' hops and Irish Moss for the last quarter of an hour.

Strain, top up, adjust the gravity, pitch the yeast, ferment, skim, rack, bottle or cask, prime, seal and store for 6 weeks or more.

Variations

1. Replace the crystal grains with 375 g (¾ lb) brown sugar.
2. Replace 500 g (1 lb) pale malt grains with 500 g (1 lb) Golden syrup.
3. Replace the flaked rice with flaked wheat.

Export Ale

Recommended original gravity 1.048–1.052 20 litres (4 gallons).

2.5 kg (5 lb) Pale malt grains
500 g (1 lb) crystal grains
500 g (1 lb) flaked maize
90 g (3 oz) 'Golding' hops
30 g (1 oz) 'Northern Brewer' hops
20 litres (4 gallons) hard water
Irish Moss
Invert sugar syrup as necessary
Ale yeast

Mash at 65.5°C (150°F). Boil the wort with two-thirds of the 'Goldings' and the 'Northern Brewer' hops. Add three-quarters of the rest of the 'Goldings' and the Irish Moss for the last quarter hour.

Strain, top up, adjust the gravity, pitch the activated yeast, ferment, skim, add the remainder of the hops for the last 2 days of the fermentation, rack, bottle, prime, seal and store for 3 months.

Variation

Replace all or some of the hops with hop pellets or dry hop with hop pellets – 'Golding' type. Keep the hop rate high.

Drawing a pint of draught bitter

Brown Ale

Recommended original gravity 1.034–1.036
20 litres (4 gallons).

1.5 kg (3 lb) pale malt grains	60 g (2 oz) 'Northdown' hops
500 g (1 lb) crystal malt grains	20 litres (4 gallons) softish water
250 g ($\frac{1}{2}$ lb) chocolate malt grains	Irish Moss
	Ale yeast
250 g ($\frac{1}{2}$ lb) flaked wheat	Lactose to sweeten if required

Mash at 60°C (140°F). Boil the wort with all the hops and Irish Moss for three-quarters of an hour.

Strain, top up, cool, adjust the gravity, pitch the yeast, ferment, skim, rack, bottle or cask, prime, seal and store for 3 weeks or more.

Dry Stout

Recommended original gravity 1.040–1.044
20 litres (4 gallons).

2.5 kg (5 lb) pale malt grains	90 g (3 oz) 'Northdown' hops
500 g (1 lb) crystal malt grains	20 litres (4 gallons) soft water
250 g ($\frac{1}{2}$ lb) chocolate malt grains	Irish Moss
	Brown invert sugar syrup as necessary
250 g ($\frac{1}{2}$ lb) black malt grains	Stout yeast
250 g ($\frac{1}{2}$ lb) flaked oats	

Mash at 65°C (149°F). Boil the wort with the Irish Moss and hops for three-quarters of an hour.

Strain, top up, adjust the gravity, pitch the yeast, ferment, skim, stir the wort each day to ensure a complete fermentation, rack bottle, prime, seal and store for 6 weeks.

Lager

Recommended original gravity 1.040–1.044
20 litres (4 gallons).

2. 5 kg (5 lb) pale malt or lager malt if available	20 litres (4 gallons) soft water
	White invert sugar syrup as necessary
500 g (1 lb) flaked maize or rice	Lager yeast (Carlsbergensis)
90 g (3 oz) 'Hallertau' or 'Saaz' hops	

Mash at 55°C (131°F) for half an hour, then at 60°C (140°F) for half an hour, then at 65°C (149°F) for half an hour, then cool to 60°C (140°F) and maintain to end point.

Strain, sparge and boil with the hops for three-quarters of an hour.

Strain, top up, cool, adjust gravity, pitch an active lager yeast, pour into a fermentation vessel, fit an air lock and ferment at 9–10°C (48–50°F) if possible.

Rack, fine if necessary, bottle, prime with invert sugar syrup, seal and store for 3 months.

There are various methods of mashing lager malts. The one given is the simplest and is a golden lager.

A ploughman's lunch

Glossary

Activated yeast: When purchased, yeast is always in a dormant state. It becomes active after it is placed in a solution containing fruit acid and sugar. This process usually takes about 24 hours.

Campden tablet: The trade name for sodium metabisulphite. It is a strong but safe bactericide and anti-oxidant, especially when mixed with citric acid in water. Widely used as a preservative and preventer of browning (oxidation).

Carbon dioxide: A colourless, tasteless and harmless gas given off during fermentation.

Dry: A lack of sweetness in a wine or beer. The opposite of sweet.

Fermentation: The action of yeast in converting fruit sugars into alcohol and carbon dioxide.

Fermentation - on - the - pulp: Fermenting the fruit juice or sugars in the presence of the crushed fruit.

Ferment-on: Continuing the fermentation after the pulp has been strained out and discarded; also after extra sugar has been added.

Ferment-out: Continuing the fermentation until the yeast has converted all the sugar to alcohol and carbon dioxide or has created so much alcohol that it is prevented from creating more. The end of fermentation.

Fine: The addition of an agent to a wine or beer that coagulates the suspended particles and takes them to the bottom of the container, leaving the wine or beer bright and clear.

Hydrometer: A simple instrument, like a thermometer in appearance, used in Homebrew for measuring the quantity of sugar in a liquid.

Mature: After a wine or beer has been made it needs a period of time while it reaches the level at which it tastes best.

Metric measures: In the recipes the metric measures are not direct equivalents of Imperial measures. Use metric or Imperial but *not* a combination of both.

Must: A watery liquid containing fruit acids and sugars as well as fruit, vegetable, flower, leaf, herb, cereal or spice essences or pulp before the yeast is added to begin the process of fermentation into wine.

Pectic enzyme: An agent sold under such names as Pectinol, Pectolase, Pectozyme, etc. When added to a fruit must it dissolves the pectin thus improving juice extraction and preventing pectin haze in the wine.

Rack: The process of removing clear or clearing wine or beer from its sediment. Often performed with the aid of a siphon.

Sediment: Particles of pulp and yeast cells, etc., that settle on the bottom of a container after fermentation of wine or beer. If not soon removed it imparts a foul smell and taste to the beverage.

Specific gravity: The weight of a given volume of a liquid compared with the same volume of water at 15°C (59°F). In Homebrew the weight is mostly sugar and can be measured with a hydrometer.

Sulphite solution: Water in which sodium metabisulphite is dissolved. Used for sterilising equipment and ingredients. See Campden tablet.

Wort: A solution of malt sugars and hop oils and essences before the yeast is added to begin the process of fermentation into beer.

Index

PDO 83-1137